1. The Right to be Heard

An overview

Introduction

This is the first of 12 papers in a series drawing on Oxfam GB's global programme of work on the theme of 'the right to be heard'. The focus of this series of papers is on how the right to be heard can strengthen the participation of people in poverty in formulating public policy, and enable them to hold decision-makers accountable. The other Oxfam themes are the right to a sustainable livelihood, the right to basic services, the right to life and security, and the right to equity. Together, these themes provide an integrated rights-based approach to Oxfam GB's core purpose of overcoming poverty and suffering.

The right to be heard is about the right to be an active participant in political processes; it is about being able to speak up and be listened to by those in power. Put a different way, it is about enabling people to actively draw on their civil and political rights to achieve their social, economic, and cultural rights. It is about finding ways to ensure that governance structures are responsive to the needs and wishes of poor people. These papers touch on some elements of how this can be achieved.

Some of the issues and challenges illustrated in these papers about the right to be heard include:

- establishing legal identity and citizenship;

- developing personal power in terms of confidence and self-esteem;

- developing collective power that enables the individual voice to be amplified and projected;

- increasing transparency and accountability of governments and institutions;
- developing a state that is capable and responsive to the needs and priorities of its citizens;
- changing the attitudes and beliefs that underlie poverty, discrimination, and prejudice.

Together, these issues concern the development of societies that take seriously the possibility of all their citizens enjoying active citizenship, and not just the most privileged.

These papers attempt to show how poor and marginalised people can become powerful enough to break through the material, organisational, systemic, and psychological barriers and obstacles that prevent them from being heard.

The context of poverty and inequality

There are still 1.4 billion people in the world today living on less than $1.25 a day.[1] Set this alongside increasing levels of inequality both between and within countries, and the global relevance of the right to be heard is clear. A girl born in Norway, for example, is likely to live until she is 82 years old, with good education and health care, while her counterpart in Sierra Leone has a 25 per cent chance of dying before she is five and a life expectancy of just 42 years.[2] If she stays in school until secondary level, she will be one of only 20 per cent of girls who do so.

However, statistics alone cannot give a realistic insight into why poverty occurs and what factors cause and perpetuate it. The dollar a day definition of poverty is still in widespread use, and enables comparisons to be made between and within countries. But this measure does not on its own tell you about the extent of poverty, since people's needs for income vary depending on their circumstances and context. Simple income-based definitions do not tell you, for example, whether the income is adequate to meet the actual needs of the individual or family, or whether they are able to make use of the income to address their needs. Poverty is affected by what choices are available in practice, and whether the individual or family is able to make their choices freely. People need access to goods, services (including health care and education), and potential sources of livelihood to change their situation. Culture, the attitudes and prejudices of others, and the power structures within which people live affect their choices, as does their vulnerability to sudden changes of circumstance such as illness or extreme climatic events.

It is for this reason that poverty is now often defined in non-monetary ways.[3] Vulnerability, powerlessness, and isolation are now considered to be as significant in understanding the dynamics of poverty as lack of income or food. For example, the UK government's Department for International Development (DFID)'s 'sustainable livelihoods framework'[4] includes human and social capital alongside financial capital and other assets.

Looking at it the other way round, what do people need in order not to be poor? They need a means of livelihood which is at least sustainable in the short term. They need basic services such as education, health care, and water. They need security and protection. They must be able to be active citizens and to be treated equally as citizens whatever their gender, race, age, ability, or culture. They also need the power to inform and influence the decisions that most affect them, and the confidence and knowledge to be able to do so.

People fall into poverty when one or more of these elements goes wrong. Their livelihood becomes unviable, or their health deteriorates and they lack the social ties, backed up by economic capacity, to sustain them; or their security evaporates, perhaps because of civil war or some kind of disaster, or relationship break-up; or there is a sharp increase in the price of food and energy, and they are suddenly facing very different circumstances. In these situations, people often lose the ability to make their voices heard and influence what happens, and they may have no say and no means to hold anyone to account.

Once they are poor, people stay in poverty partly because their rights are not achieved or respected. They may belong to a social group that has little status or collective voice in society and no control over the decisions that get made about it. Initiatives that address this lack of voice, as well as the more tangible aspects of their situation, can make a big difference to people's ability to achieve greater well-being and get out of poverty.

Poverty and power: why does the right to be heard matter?

Poverty and inequality often persist because unaccountable governments and ineffective institutions block progress towards adopting and implementing pro-poor policies. Many government agencies and other institutions continue to make decisions that fail to respond to the needs of poor and marginalised people; systems of justice are often inaccessible to poor people. They are often excluded from forums where decicions are made on issues that directly affect their welfare. There are many places where women, in particular, are not consulted or included.

People elected or appointed to positions of power rarely represent the interests of poor people. These are issues of governance – the rules of the game and the structures that oversee and implement those rules. Structures and systems thus impinge on the lives of poor people and power is exercised over them in many ways, both overt and more subtle.

Through the papers in this series there is a constant thread concerning power and power relations, including the power created by taking action. In thinking about what work can and should be done to support poor women and men in realising their rights and voice in decisions that affect them, it is useful to look at the whole spectrum of power and power relations, and not just at the visible power relations and formal power relationships that are perhaps more familiar targets for advocacy in trying to make change happen. It is clear that there is a wide spectrum of starting points – whether geographic, or in terms of the kinds of spaces where power operates such as public forums and institutions, informal social interactions, mass mobilisations, and so on. Only strategies which address the many-layered nature of power can lead to effective, sustainable change. The task looks very different in different contexts and historical moments; and has to be specific to the gender power relations and other power inequalities.

Power takes many forms and can be found as much in the nature of relationships as in formal structures and institutions. There is the positive 'power from within' of confidence and self-esteem, the kind of invisible power that can transform the individual from passive or unquestioning to assertive and active. Then there is 'power with'. This is the power of organisation, creating both informal and formal spaces where individual power can be brought together and amplified to engage with power-holders and make effective demands. The Honduras paper is a good example of 'power with', where women *maquila* workers, who had very little power as individuals, were able to improve their situation by joining together and challenging those with 'power over' them. 'Power with' also finds expression in the power of mobilisation, activism, and movements, within or in relation to existing formal or hidden power structures, or as independent spaces of engagement. Examples of this can be found in the papers on the Global Call to Action against Poverty and the *Wada Na Todo* ('Keep Your Promises') movement in India. These camapaigns used tools such as citizens' report cards and tribunals to engage diverse groups in successfully raising their voices in national and local campaigning.

> **Power**
>
> Power is often understood merely in terms of one person's ability to achieve a desired end, with or without the consent of others, but it comes in at least four different forms:
>
> - Power *over*: the power of the strong over the weak. This power is often hidden – for example, what elites manage to keep off the table of political debate.
>
> - Power *to*: meaning the capability to decide actions and carry them out.
>
> - Power *with*: collective power, through organisation, solidarity, and joint action.
>
> - Power *within*: personal self-confidence, often linked to culture, religion, or other aspects of collective identity, which influence what thoughts and actions appear legitimate or acceptable.[5]

Becoming full and active citizens is a journey people make. They start in different places, and move at different speeds depending on their context and life experience; they can move backwards as well as forwards on the road. There are obstacles and roadblocks, as well as things that can propel an individual or group forwards. These vary according to context. The papers in this series illustrate action that is being or has been taken in a range of contexts, drawing on Oxfam GB's experience of working with different organisations in 13 countries. They exemplify some of the personal and systemic issues and challenges in working to make the voices of poor and marginalised people heard by people in positions of power. Such issues include:

Legal citizenship rights and inclusion

If you have no right to a legal identity, or your legal identity has stigma attached, it is very difficult to claim your rights or make your voice heard. The Peru paper in this series tells of a successful campaign to address such an issue, in relation to the rights of children to be registered at birth. Legal identity, however, is not necessarily enough to give you full citizenship rights. The Guatemala and Indonesia papers show two different ways of using 'power with' and 'power to' in addressing this issue. In Guatemala, women are using the indigenous justice system to tackle the impunity culture of the formal state system that has prevented women accessing full citizenship rights in the face of high levels of violence. In Indonesia, poor local communities, and particularly women, are using participatory poverty assessments as a mechanism for tackling exclusion from local services and governance.

Developing personal power, self-confidence, and self-esteem

Accessing your rights as a citizen may be prevented because you are afraid, or lack the confidence to claim them. On a personal level, these are significant obstacles which can only be overcome by the person concerned, though there are many things that can help the individual in this part of the journey. Knowing you are not the only one facing the challenge can make a big difference. Changes in personal power are often closely linked with actions that also strengthen 'power with' or 'power to'. In Bangladesh, a programme with indigenous *adibashi* people led to women taking leadership for the first time, and speaking out within traditional governance structures. In Georgia, local community members were able to develop the skills and confidence to participate in formal budget-monitoring processes in local government. These are some ways in which 'power within' can be nurtured and strengthened, allowing positive changes to take place.

Collective organisation

Collective voice is more effective than individuals speaking out on their own. In general, the more voices the better, as these papers show. The Global Call to Action against Poverty (GCAP) involved millions of people in mass protests, raising collective voice, and had significant successes in changing policies and promises on aid, trade, and development, and articulating the voices of poor and marginalised people. In India, the *Wa Na Todo* movement mobilised thousands of people to demand change from the government in a range of areas such as health and education. In Malawi, local-level awareness and capacity and mobilisation were achieved though organising training and village-level discussion groups. In the UK, it was possible for disparate groups of poor and marginalised people to be brought together to influence government policy.

Transparency and accountability

But just making a lot of noise about an issue may not achieve results. Good solutions to the problems of an absence of rights and capabilities require accurate information, which is not always easily available. The paper on India shows how the introduction of a freedom of information act, after much campaigning and the mobilisation of many people, was a major step forward in supporting people's right to be heard. Equally, technical work such as budget monitoring can be very useful in providing a tangible hook for programme work and an entry point through 'power to' for engaging with formal power structures. However, this needs to be in conjunction with advocacy, awareness-raising, and economic-literacy work rather than on its own, as the paper on budget monitoring in Malawi demonstrates.

Even when policy change is achieved, it is not sufficient unless that policy is implemented effectively, by people and institutions with the required skills and capacities, and unless it is given the resources necessary for the changes to reach people on the ground. Therefore accountability also needs to be part of the mix, whether through citizens monitoring government decisions and actions (for example on budget allocations), or through campaigning and other forms of collective action that demand account to be given (as seen in the papers on Malawi, India, and GCAP).

Work with power-holders: responsive states

Lasting change requires more than just change on the part of poor and marginalised people and their organisations. Change is also needed in duty-bearers' responsiveness to citizens – these duty-bearers are usually the government ministers or officials who are so often the holders and wielders of 'power over'. Constructive proposals for change can be made, but if they meet a blank wall of unresponsiveness, poor people's lives will be no better for it. It is often necessary to work on both the 'supply' and 'demand' sides of governance – with both the institutions of the state and with citizens and their organisations. In Indonesia, as well as working with poor communities to develop knowledge and confidence, the Driving Change project worked with partners to build relationships with local and district governments, and in some cases to tackle unjust and corrupt practices. In the UK the Get Heard project deliberately set out to demonstrate a methodology for getting poor people to engage with power-holders who had expressed a willingness to listen but did not know how.

Attitudes and beliefs

It is also necessary to work at the level of those attitudes and beliefs that underpin how people act and interact, in order for accountability to be meaningful. These may be the attitudes and beliefs about poor people (for example, where poor people are seen as 'deserving' or 'undeserving') held by many people who are not poor. Or they may be the attitudes and beliefs held by people who control resource allocation, which may allow self-serving behaviour to take precedence over behaviour that delivers just and equitable use of resources. Examples of this can be seen in the paper on corruption, which explores ways of addressing the issue through some of the apparently tangential but essential cultural and attitudinal changes that enable people to have higher expectations of probity and accountability from power-holders.

The right to be heard

The case studies in this series can be located in different places on the diagram below, which shows how the different aspects of the right to be heard outlined earlier, and the range of issues identified above, fit together. Most of the examples can fit in more than one place. The kinds of changes required for poor and marginalised people to have an effective voice demand action at all points in the model.

The dimensions of voice with power

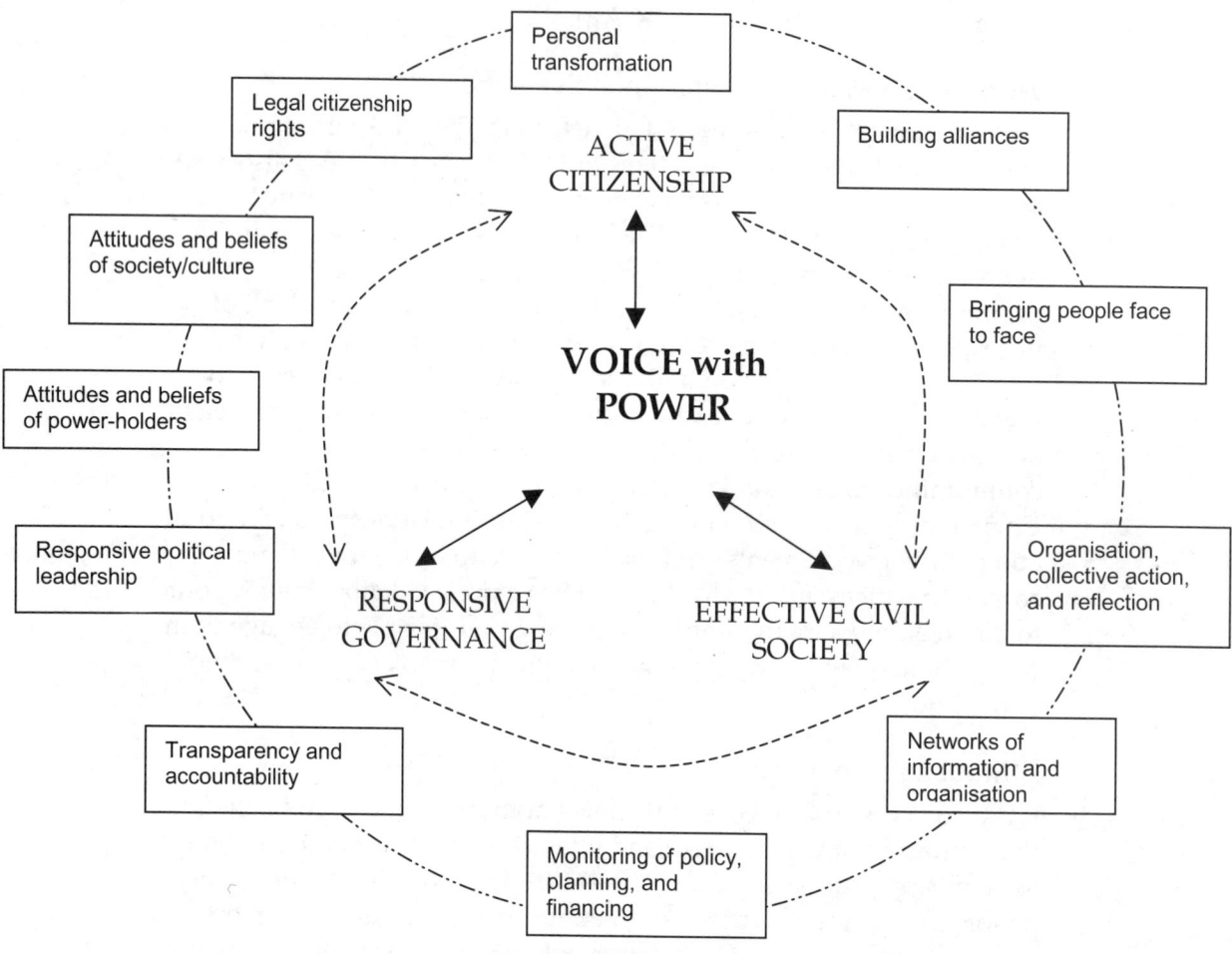

How can people be supported to make their voices heard?

Support to poor and marginalised people can be direct – through provision of finance and skills development to enable effective organisation, or activities that develop confidence and self-esteem. But in addition to this, there is much that can be done, less directly, to strengthen the elements of an environment that will make it more likely for people to be heard and responded to. For example, one difficulty encountered in attempts to embed 'voice' and participation into formal systems is that it is all too easy for well-intentioned attempts at inclusion to become tokenistic. Spaces that are successfully opened up for inclusion often get 'captured' by elites and lead to little real change for poor people. Such attempts can unintentionally reduce the space for voice, since power-holders can then claim that the change has already been made. There is a useful role, therefore, for supportive action to prevent 'capture', and to develop capacity for receptiveness among people in power such as those in local government.

Another element of an enabling environment is sensitivity to gender issues, and to the issues of other groups of people whose voices are often not heard because they are marginalised in some way in society. It can help if the people who are not the ones missing out highlight the absence of the issues of marginalised groups in power structures; this kind of action is particularly supportive if these attitudes can be constructively challenged, so that there is greater awareness and understanding of the issues and more possibility for developing a responsive attitude.

Conclusion

There are a number of lessons and general recommendations from this series of papers, that others seeking to make similar changes can learn from, though there is no claim to have all the answers. These lessons need to be adapted and implemented, amplified and reinterpreted many times over; they also need to be linked up 'vertically' with work designed to have a greater impact on underlying rules, structures, institutions, attitudes, and beliefs. Adequate recognition of the points below will mean that poor and marginalised people can be supported to lobby for changes in their situation.

1   **Recognise that change is long-term.** Encouraging voice and supporting active citizenship is not a quick fix; it can only happen over a number of years. Institutionalising the participation of poor men and women as part of government structures remains a challenge. Regular follow-up action is needed to consolidate learning, as well as forward planning in order to institutionalise change.

2   **Understand that attitudinal change is important.** Attitudes about the use of power and accountability are a key entry point for NGOs into work on governance and accountability. A culture of respect and inclusiveness promotes the participation of marginalised groups in decision-making.

3   **Put local priorities first.** For any large network to be successful in ensuring poor people's right to be heard, priorities must be built from local, regional, and national contexts and then draw on international frameworks. Local communities have lots of energy and know the details of the issues that affect them. What they lack are mechanisms to effectively engage and hold their representatives accountable.

4   **Work at a number of levels and build alliances.** Such alliances must be built with people in poverty, with people in power, and with those who have the responsibility for implementing policy. The work also needs to happen at local, national, and international levels. The links between popular mobilisation, awareness-raising, policy change, and implementation are important. Adequate attention must be given to issues of implementation as well as policy change. Successful alliances are key to a successful project.

5   **Bring people face to face.** Formal power-holders and policy makers often have limited direct contact with poor and marginalised people. There is plenty more scope for bringing people face to face; such encounters, if well handled, can be very powerful.

6   **Use a range of strategies to build success.** Information, research, and training are all important. Many of the papers show how capacity-building of local-level organisations is often crucial in achieving the desired impact. A number of projects used participatory methodologies. The methods used matter: disempowering methodology, however unintentional, can invalidate the best-laid plans; empowering methodology contributes positively to change.

7   **Take different perspectives into account.** The national framework has to take account of the perspectives and voices of groups that are marginalised in social and economic terms, as well as groups cutting across gender and age (for example, children) in order to seek their support and build their capacity. The different needs and views of different groups must be accounted for.

8   **Acknowledge gender differences.** Paying good attention to gender differences and gender power relations can enable more effective change to happen.

9   **Use the right language.** It is possible to create excitement and enthusiasm for issues such as health, education, and even budgeting. The key is to articulate these in a language that people understand and want to respond to.

10   **Monitor and evaluate projects.** This shows how far bringing policy makers face to face with those who are affected by the policies they design can influence these policies, and what else has an influence on change processes.

11   **Recognise that international agencies can play an advocacy role.** They can influence the United Nations and other donor agencies to comply with their own policies and commitments to support development projects that encourage voice. Besides building technical capacities, international agencies can play a very

significant role in building links to civil society, governments, and private-sector stakeholders inside and outside the country.

12 **Understand that NGOs are important as role models of accountability and integrity.** If NGOs successfully demonstrate good practice, this not only shows people an example of how accountability can work in action, but also lays foundations for relationships of trust and mutual respect.

Notes

[1] S. Chen and M. Revallion (2008) 'The Developing World is Poorer than we Thought, but No Less Successful in the Fight against Poverty', Policy Research Working Paper 4703, Washington DC: World Bank.

[2] D. Green and I. Allen (2008) *The Urgency of Now*, Oxford: Oxfam GB.

[3] Best-known is the thinking of Amartya Sen and Martha Nussbaum in their writing on capabilities. See A. Sen (2001) *Development as Freedom*, Oxford: Oxford University Press, and M. Nussbaum (2000) *Women and Human Development: The Capabilities Approach*, Cambridge: Cambridge University Press.

[4] See National Strategies for Sustainable Development (2004) 'The DFID Approach to Sustainable Livelihoods', www.nssd.net/references/SustLiveli/DFIDapproach.htm (last accessed September 2008).

[5] D. Green (2008) *From Poverty to Power*, Oxford: Oxfam GB.

Oxfam GB

Oxfam GB is a development, relief, and campaigning organisation that works with others to find lasting solutions to poverty and suffering around the world. Oxfam GB is a member of Oxfam International.

Oxfam House
John Smith Drive
Cowley
Oxford
OX4 2JY

Tel: +44.(0)1865.473727
E-mail: enquiries@oxfam.org.uk
www.oxfam.org.uk

2. A Life with Dignity

Honduran women raising voices to improve labour standards

Maquila workers in San Pedro Sula (northern Honduras) demand respect and the protection of their labour rights

This paper shows how CODEMUH (Colectiva de Mujeres Hondureñas), a grassroots women's collective in Honduras, mobilised a popular movement around labour rights in the country's textile factories, or *maquilas*. Focusing on occupational health, CODEMUH ran a campaign which included research, training, and advocacy workshops for the women themselves, building alliances locally, nationally, and internationally, and involving key journalists and the media. The paper explains the challenges and the strategies used to overcome them. It also outlines the lessons learned when women have greater capacity to advocate for changes in policy and practice at corporate and national levels.

Introduction

Honduras is one of the poorest countries in Latin America, with a per capita income of $1,260.[1] The country ranks 117th out of 177 countries in the United Nations Human Development Index. According to the World Bank, in 2006, over 50 per cent of the population lived in poverty, and around 21 per cent in extreme poverty, defined as less than $1 per day.[2]

For all these reasons, the government desperately needs investment. And the country's *maquilas* have seemed an easy route for foreign funds. The term *maquila* describes the textile factories throughout Central America that operate as part of tariff-free export-processing zones.[3]

In 2006, Honduras' 156 *maquilas* represented 36 per cent of the total manufacturing industry and 6.5 per cent of the country's gross domestic product (GDP).[4] Although they are concentrated in a relatively small number of industrial areas, the *maquilas* of Honduras have ensured that the country has reached number five as the world supplier of clothing products, and number one in the Central America and Caribbean region. The factories employ around 130,000 people.[5]

The growth of the *maquila* sector has been nurtured by public policies and special regimes that allow foreign and national investors to create and operate tax-free industrial zones on advantageous terms of trade. In efforts to attract foreign investment over the past three decades,[6] a number of laws have been approved to reduce costs, flexibilise labour, and maximise profits for investors.

The vulnerability of *maquila* workers

The positive government story of profits and competitiveness is a long way from the experience of most of the *maquila* workers.[7] The factories may have created jobs, but labour conditions are poor, workers are generally underpaid, and their rights are frequently violated. The average salary is $83 a month.[8] Many *maquilas* pay by task. This means that although a certain quota may be set in terms of how much should be achieved in eight hours, it could in fact take ten hours to meet this quota, so workers end up receiving eight hours' pay for ten hours' work. A typical quota is to iron 1,200 shirts, standing, in a nine-hour day.[9]

More than half the *maquila* employees are rural women and 70 per cent are between the ages of 18 and 25.[10] Applicants for employment are screened carefully. They are normally aged between 18 and 34. The younger the better, as they are less likely to complain. Even 14-year-olds are accepted if they say they are 16. Proof that the woman is not pregnant is demanded, and pregnancy is often a reason for firing women. As one writer notes: 'Some *maquilas* in Honduras, according to Charles Kernaghan, director of the New York-based National Labor Committee, periodically give shots of the contraceptive Depro Provera, saying it is for tetanus.'[11]

A significant proportion of the women working in *maquilas* are single mothers and the sole breadwinner in the family. They are generally forced to leave before they turn 35.[12] Because they are likely to have had less formal education than men, there are few opportunities, when they are 'retired', to move into management or other areas in the factory. Instead, they have to look for domestic work or enrol in the informal economy to survive. As a consequence, thousands of workers end up living in extreme poverty in industrial areas with no services and without enough income to find a way out.[13]

To compound these problems of vulnerability, Honduras is also a very violent country – there are more than 3,000 violent deaths a year.[14] Since 2002, more than 900 women have been killed, targeted specifically because they are women – these killings are sometimes known as 'femicides'.[15] According to ASEPROLA,[16] a non-government organisation (NGO) that works for labour rights in Central America, there seems to be a link between the increasing rates of femicides and the concentration of *maquila* factories in large urban cities. This connection is due to a combination of factors such as weak state protection of citizens, impunity, lack of arms control and regulation, inequality, poverty, and precarious living conditions that characterise the areas where large populations of vulnerable young women live.

Impact on women's health[17]

A recent study conducted by a medical specialist team, including doctors from Honduras and Mexico, provides evidence of health implications for women working in the *maquilas*. Based on a sample of 450 cases, including 270 women and 180 men, up to 75 per cent of women working in *maquilas* show symptoms of fatigue caused mainly by extensive working hours – up to 12 hours or more on a daily basis. Sixty-seven per cent of women need medical attention on a regular basis to deal with respiratory diseases, allergic reactions, and musculoskeletal disease. In the survey:

92.4 per cent showed musculoskeletal disease

67.9 per cent had evidence of increased body mass index (BMI) leading to obesity and overweight

49 per cent had respiratory diseases (sinusitus, asthma, etc.)

24.5 per cent had problems of poor circulation including risk of deep-vein thrombosis

Many showed signs of stress, fatigue, and insomnia

The current Honduran Labour Code acknowledges only 44 work-related illnesses. Labour rights defence organisations are proposing to reform the Labour Code to improve its standards and to include another 241 illnesses that have been recgonised as work-related.[18]

To compete for contracts, factories try to offer high productivity and low production costs. To achieve this, working hours are extended, quotas are subcontracted to smaller factories or individuals, health and safety conditions are reduced, and labour benefits such as health care, overtime payment, meal and resting time, etc. are dramatically reduced or simply disappear through unfair contracting terms and conditions. Mostly, unions are not allowed. Only 7 per cent of the economically active population is affiliated with trade unions, down from an estimated 15 per cent in the 1960s.[19]

Those who dare to defend workers' rights are quickly fired or forced to quit. It is widely known they will end up on a blacklist shared with other factories to keep them from getting contracted within the sector again.[20] 'The employers don't want unions. When they realised we had created a union, they fired us. Our names are now written on blacklists', says Rita, a former *maquila* worker.[21]

All this despite the fact that Honduras has ratified key conventions of the International Labour Organization (ILO), committing itself to uphold three core labour standards – the prohibition of child and forced labour, the right to free association and collective bargaining, and freedom from discrimination. But ratifying an ILO convention and fully enforcing it in a proactive manner are worlds apart: violations of core labour standards can be seen in nearly every country in the world, including the most developed nations.

In 2004, Labour Minister German Leitzelar admitted that in Honduras there was a gap between legislation and reality: 'We find that the legislation is not sufficient to be able to talk about the application of these labour standards', and 'decisions in the economic arena are almost exclusively taken totally divorced from national social policy'.[22]

Because the government promotes employment policies based on cheap labour, labour-rights legal frameworks have been reformed in alignment with private-sector interests to reduce production costs and increase productivity. This means that much less public attention is paid to working conditions and little support is given to internationally recognised labour rights such as freedom of association and health and safety protocols. Public institutions usually responsible for the protection of workers' rights have been weakened because their resources have been cut and their functions and responsibilities restructured. Honduras not only lacks proper national frameworks to ensure fair and decent labour practices, but also fails to promote the effective eradication of gender discrimination in the workplace.

In addition, the government is pushing through reforms that would allow factories to hire up to 30 per cent of their workers on temporary contracts. If passed, *maquila* employers could save $90m over three years – but for the workers, it would mean no job security, paid leave, or social security.[23]

There are few sanctions when things go wrong: the 2007 report of the Inter-American Human Rights Commission on the state of labour rights in the *maquila* sector in Central America noted that there are few resources and possibilities for monitoring the sector. For example, if workers denounce violations and demand inspections there is no legally binding period of time in which action must be taken. This means either that inspections never take place, or the company is given time to fix the issue – and possibly fire those who demanded the inspection in the first place. In addition, when they do arrive, public inspectors don't interview workers. Conclusions and recommendations tend to be based on information provided by the employers and factory reports and files. Even if they were to find fault, the highest fine that a factory in Honduras would have to pay is $260. In the end, paying a fine is cheaper for the company than changing their practice.

'I was fired because I was injured'

'My task was to lift boxes filled with harnesses, to pack and seal them. I would pick them up from the floor up to the table to complete the packing, that is how I hurt my back from doing drastic movements for 12 hours every day, bending myself and lifting boxes all day in a repetitive way', explains Meredith, a *maquila* worker who was fired because of health conditions.

'During the nine months I worked in the factory, the pain kept increasing and the doctor [factories have in-house clinics] applied injections every day but I was not allowed to go to a hospital because he [the doctor] had been instructed to give sick leave permission only to women who had haemorrhages, miscarriages, or things like that'.

Meredith was finally fired, and now she is going for medical treatment at the social security hospital, she has been diagnosed with herniated discs and other associated problems. She is currently waiting for surgery. This is just one of many examples in which corporations and the state fail to protect basic labour rights.

Oxfam Honduras team

Women organising

Colectiva de Mujeres Hondureñas (CODEMUH – 'Collective of Honduran Women') began as a feminist grassroots movement in the urban area of Choloma in the late 1980s. It was created by a group of women who wanted to bring about changes in Honduran society regarding women's rights and gender equality. Over the years, CODEMUH prioritised women's rights in the areas of labour, sexual and reproductive health, and gender violence. CODEMUH is made up of a network of *maquila* workers and other women who have direct experience of the unfair conditions and disadvantages of working in the factories.

CODEMUH has an executive board and a technical and administrative structure. Twenty-three women work full-time, many of whom have been *maquila* workers in the past, and there is also a network of 1,000 female volunteers and activists organised into 32 neighbourhood groups that include *maquila* workers, students, and so on.

CODEMUH helps to organise working women, strengthening their self-esteem and confidence. It provides counselling and support on an individual and collective basis, and holds workshops and training sessions in neighbourhoods and even inside the *maquilas*. On the advocacy side, it researches, writes, and publishes information and supports women whose rights have been violated by taking their claims either to the *maquila* responsible, or to court.

Advocacy, as a tool, has been used by CODEMUH since 2000, but it was not until 2003, when the organisation started to realise its potential, that it decided to use it in a more systematic, planned, and organised way. In 2004 an internal training programme was implemented which aimed to enhance the skills of women members who had shown potential in leading lobby activities, dealing with the press, or negotiating with *maquila* owners or public authorities.

With Oxfam support and training, and with the Institute for Social Research and Advocacy (an Oxfam partner NGO) taking CODEMUH through the process, an 'Advocacy School' was implemented over nine months. It combined workshops and fieldwork to apply tools and knowledge on lobbying and advocacy work. It worked with 25 women, mainly from CODEMUH's technical and directorial teams, to build their skills and also to generate institutional debate about CODEMUH's vision and agenda for the future. Volunteers and activists who were working in the *maquilas* participated in other workshops, mainly at the weekends, or during the night when they were not working. Although CODEMUH has been able to get attention and support to carry out some workshops on violence against women and sexual and reproductive rights, *maquila* owners would never allow employees to get training on labour rights.

Developing skills to empower other women

Nicole, a former *maquila* worker, started to get involved with CODEMUH in 2003 when a community facilitator came to her neighbourhood to form a women's group and offer workshops on gender, self-esteem, and labour rights. Today, Nicole works full-time at CODEMUH as a trainer.

'I can see the changes in women as they are trained, as they share experiences and learn new things', she says. 'As women we are not very good at speaking, or at least we have not had practice, and this is one of the strongest changes that I have seen. I don't expect women to be able to address a big audience or talk in public, but they do now speak out in places where they feel secure, when they can trust people, or when they feel they have to get something off their chests'.[24]

Putting theory into practice: a campaign on occupational health

Two of the outcomes of this training process were the development of a three-year advocacy strategy, and the organisation of an advocacy team formed by seven women to shape and implement CODEMUH's campaign on occupational health.

The campaign aimed to raise awareness and influence *maquila* owners, public institutions, the media, and society in general about women's working conditions and respect for human and labour rights. CODEMUH wanted working women to see themselves as key agents of social and economic development. It also aimed to enhance their capacity to air their views and demand respect for their rights, particularly regarding health and safety conditions in the factories.

The campaign was launched in 2004. It involved four phases. In the first phase, CODEMUH developed research to provide evidence of health and safety-related risks at work and to support the advocacy agenda. In the second phase, the results of these studies were presented to the public and a two-fold lobbying strategy was delivered, targeting decision-makers in the government and the private sector and developing a more solid relationship with key journalists from local and national media. At this point the campaign had gained support from at least five civil-society organisations, including labour unions and some faith-based groups. Together they formed the Alianza para la Protección Laboral ('Alliance for Labour Rights Protection'). The campaign was also linked to a labour rights regional campaign bringing together women workers' organisations from five Central American countries to focus on working and health conditions inside maquila factories,[25] and to the Global 'Make Trade Fair' Campaign on Women's Labour Rights. It helped provide further support and backing for these campaigns, attracting global attention to labour issues and putting international pressure on governments, transnational companies, and national *maquila* owners.

> **Going public and media coverage**
>
> On 1 May, Labour Day, unions in Latin America traditionally march through the streets of major cities. CODEMUH felt that it was time to take part in this public demonstration, and decided to join the march. CODEMUH also decided to give a speech to send out a message not only to *maquila* owners but also to society as a whole about working conditions inside *maquilas* and the impact on women's rights, particularly on occupational health. In May 2006, for the first time ever in San Pedro Sula in north Honduras, a women's organisation marched alongside labour unions. This attracted a lot of attention from the media and society. Historically, the march had been dominated by male trade unionists. CODEMUH's group turned out to be the largest and best-organised representation. The women's speech at the closing event was agreed to be one of the clearest, most focused, and most inspiring, and received extensive national media coverage.[26]

CODEMUH continued to participate in public demonstrations in 2007 and 2008, denouncing abuses and presenting proposals to change labour policies and practices. The way national media is approaching these issues is changing, and now people have access to more objective analysis of labour and health issues related to working conditions inside the *maquilas*. Conducting quality research has helped to back up CODEMUH's proposals. Below are some examples of how national media is now approaching the issue:

'The research revealed that 58 per cent of interviewed female workers are not included in the social security scheme; this reflects that within the *maquila* sector the application of our labour legislation is deficient.'

La Tribuna Newspaper, January 2007[27]

'The proposal demands an increase in indemnity amounts for work-related accidents and an increase in sanctions on entrepreneurs that fail to comply with national labour laws and international agreements.'

La Prensa Newspaper, March 2008[28]

'*Maquila* managers took advantage of the Independence holiday to shut down the factory [for good]...without complying with the labour rights duties to the employees. 250 employees have been affected by this; most of them are women.' [i.e. they lost their jobs and did not get severance pay].

Tiempo Digital News, September 2006[29]

In the third phase, key campaign messages were disseminated by means of radio spots and newspapers. There were educational and mobilisation activities at community level with women working in *maquilas*. Thirty-four new community groups were given the skills to communicate their messages and participate in the different activities. Workshops continued to be held with wider audiences to share the findings of the research and raise awareness about human and labour rights in the garment sector. In the last phase, media coverage was monitored to assess to what extent the approach of the media had changed and what key stakeholders were saying about women's labour rights in the apparel industry.

Reaction and counter-reaction: pro-*maquila* messages

By looking at the media coverage and monitoring people's participation in radio programmes, televised debates, and workshops, it was obvious that the campaign had increased public attention to occupational health issues in the *maquilas*. As general opinion and the mass media started to shift in favour of CODEMUH's campaign, the Alliance for Labour Rights Protection also gathered support, and more civil-society organisations started to exert pressure on the government and on private companies.

The private sector counter-reacted with a media campaign of its own. Their campaign emphasised the economic contributions of the *maquilas* to the country's economy through exports and employment.

For a few weeks every radio spot for CODEMUH was followed by a pro-*maquila* message. The media continued to cover CODEMUH's activities and proposals, so the private-sector campaign put pressure on journalists to stop covering CODEMUH's events and/or producing any information related to the campaign objectives.[30]

Even though media coverage on campaign activities was reduced as a result of this pressure, the Alliance for Labour Rights Protection was able to influence the Honduran Congress. It demanded that the Secretary of State for Labour start reviewing the Honduran Labour Code, particularly a chapter on occupational health and safety.

Shifting power relations: what has been achieved

Opening up space and pressuring authorities to review the occupational health and safety chapter in the Labour Code has been a big step, even though it is taking time and there are new barriers and continuing strong opposition from powerful political and economical elites in Honduras.

Other outcomes of the campaign are perceived to be equally important for working women in Honduras. CODEMUH has carried out surveys[31] and reflection sessions with women workers and allies to explore to what extent the campaign has helped to influence collective ideas and beliefs regarding labour rights. These found that:

- The Ministry of Labour started to implement some health and safety monitoring visits, although factory owners are still warned before they take place, and these visits are not systematic. This showed that denunciation of abuses and the claiming of rights by women and pressure groups like CODEMUH and its allies can lead to government and corporate action. Monitoring visits are a proxy indicator that the Honduran government and the private sector are recognising health and safety issues.

- Labour law reforms have been taken all the way to Congress, but are still waiting for approval, which could take many months.

- Some factories are improving some of the working conditions on safety and occupational health, although this is not systematic. Once again, pressure from civil society and workers has resulted in positive actions at various levels. Stronger law enforcement will be needed to achieve greater impact.

- Occupational health and safety issues have entered the public domain. Individuals, particularly women workers, have become more aware of the problems, the implications, and their own rights.

- There is greater recognition of CODEMUH's and other women's organisations' legitimacy to represent working women's rights.

Formerly, government officials and even labour unions would not recognise the voice of CODEMUH as representative, but after the campaign, CODEMUH has become an active and respected stakeholder in the labour-rights debate.

- Working women say that the attitudes and practices of inspectors, judges, and lawyers are slowly changing. More attention is being given to labour-rights violations as well as to following them up in order to resolve them.

- CODEMUH has increased the number and type of alliances with both public- and private-sector stakeholders working on health and justice issues at national and regional level.

The overall achievement is that the terms of the debate and power relations have been changed. The campaign has also led women to recognise when their rights are being infringed: 'If five years ago a *maquila* worker had been asked about labour conditions she would have replied the conditions were very good; they [*maquila* workers] were not aware of the responsibilities of *maquila* owners and investors regarding working conditions – now more of them know those responsibilities and their rights', said Maria Luisa Regalado, CODEMUH's co-ordinator.[32]

Changing policy is slow, because it is highly political and corporate interests are affected. These are the challenges for advocacy work when state institutions are weak. Many of the positive outcomes of the work concern changes in the ideas and beliefs of various stakeholders, from working women who now know more about their rights and are willing to say when they are being violated, to public officials who are more responsive to women's demands, as well as government and the private sector who recognise organisations such as CODEMUH as valid and legitimate groups that give voice to women in defence of their rights.

Recommendations

Drawing lessons from CODEMUH's experience in developing capacity to lead advocacy and campaigning actions, some key recommendations can be made:

- Advocacy work on women rights, either at local or national level, will eventually lead to interaction with male-dominated structures in government, the private sector, or the media. Therefore, any advocacy-training programme for women's organisations needs to be aware that building women's confidence and leadership skills and ensuring that their voices are heard is as important as developing technical skills and knowledge. This can often be done by also building the capacity of local-level groups.

- Advocacy and campaigning work needs to work at many levels to keep pressure on targets coming from different points; organisations working in developing advocacy capacities can increase their effectiveness if they look at individual skills and potential capacities to complement each other and achieve a mix of strengths within the group. For example, women may not want to speak in public, but could be very persuasive as lobbyists.

- Analysis of context, power, and media coverage should be undertaken regularly to measure to what extent advocacy and campaign strategies are effective and to what extent changes are taking place.

- Advocacy on women's rights needs to incorporate strategies to influence ideas and beliefs. Mass media can play an effective role in changing the way society understands women's issues.

- Media attention to issues tends to be brief, so it is very important to understand who sets the daily information priorities and how, as well as what a journalist needs in terms of content, contacts, and time to produce a press or radio piece.

- Advocacy for women's rights needs to integrate not only women's voices and stories from within the movement, but also from other sectors in society. Mobilising other women to air their views, even if they were not *maquila* workers, proved to be a very powerful way to influence public opinion.

- Alliance building from local to international level can be necessary and is very effective, but it is hard and complex work. Understanding the added value of an alliance is very important in order to judge its effectiveness and relevance. It is also important to understand when these alliances are not working, and to have strategies planned for disengagement, to reduce risks.

- Strong and sound research carried out by qualified researchers and institutions is very important to back proposals but also to build an effective relationship with key allies, particularly with journalists and other media stakeholders.

- Besides building technical capacities, international NGOs can play a very significant role in building links with civil society, governments, and private-sector stakeholders inside and outside the country.

- Women's-rights advocacy work can be a long-term process. Funding organisations need to be prepared to support and accompany them beyond the project itself.

Notes

[1] US Department of State (2008) 'Background note: Honduras', www.state.gov/r/pa/ei/bgn/1922.htm (last accessed September 2008).

[2] The German Federal Ministry for Economic Cooperation and Development (2006) 'Countries and regions – Partner countries – Honduras – Cooperation', www.bmz.de/en/countries/partnercountries/honduras/zusammenarbeit.html (last accessed September 2008).

[3] A *maquiladora* was originally a miller who charged a *maquila,* or 'miller's portion' for processing other people's grain.

[4] Central Bank of Honduras (2007) 'Actividad Maquiladora en Honduras Año 2006 y Expectativas para el Año 2007', Tegucigalpa, p. 7, www.bch.hn/download/maquila/actividad_maquiladora_2006_exp2007.pdf (last accessed October 2008).

[5] War on Want (n.d.) 'Factory closures place thousands of livelihoods at risk', London, www.waronwant.org/Factory%20Closures%20Place%20 Thousands%20of%20Livelihoods%20at%20Risk+10644.twl (last accessed September 2008).

[6] Four legal reforms and special decrees have paved the way to *maquilas* to enjoy fiscal exemptions: Freetrade Zones (ZOLI) in 1976, Temporary Imports Regime (RIT) in 1984, Industrial Processing Zone (ZIP) in 1987, US– Dominican Republic and Central American Free Trade Agreement (US–DRCAFTA) in 2005. From International Labor Organization (ILO) and CODEMUH's reports.

[7] On 18 July 2007, CODEMUH presented a report on 'Women's Working Conditions in the Maquila Industry' to the Inter American Human Rights Commission in Washington DC. The report presentation was followed by a Petition to the Commission to follow up on the Honduran government violations to national and international labour rights frameworks and conventions. See CODEMUH (2007) 'Report to the Inter American Human Rights Commission on Women's Working Conditions in the Maquila Industry', www.codemuh.org/index.php?option=com_content&task=view&id=21&Itemid=2 (last accessed September 2008).

[8] G. MacEoin (1999) 'Maquila neoslavery, under conditions from bad to inhuman', *National Catholic Reporter*, www.natcath.com/NCR_Online/archives/081399/081399i.htm (last accessed September 2008).

[9] G. MacEoin (1999), *op.cit.*

[10] Honduras Association of Manufacturers (2007) 'Employment Generation Report', www.ahm-honduras.com/html/datos/Empleosagosto2007.pdf (last accessed September 2008).

[11] *Ibid.*

[12] CODEMUH (2007), *op.cit.*

[13] M.A. Martinez (2003) 'Labor Laws in Honduras', Tegucigalpa: Oxfam International.

[14] *La Tribuna* (2008) 'Honduras, el pais mas violento de America Latina', www.latribuna.hn/news/45/ARTICLE/28916/2008-03-03.html (last accessed September 2008); RCT (2008) 'President takes action against the world's highest homicide rate', press release from the Rehabilitation and Research Center for Torture Victims, www.rct.dk/Link_menu/News/2008/Murder_rate_Honduras.aspx (last accessed September 2008).

[15] Proceso Digital (2008) 'Demandan esclarecer femicidios y respetar derechos de mujeres en Honduras', 8 March, www.proceso.hn/2008/ 03/08/Nacionales/Demandan.esclarecer.femicidios/4530.html (last accessed September 2008).

[16] ASEPROLA (2007) 'Impunidad y explotacion laboral alientan el femicidio', press release, www.aseprola.org/leer.php/82 (last accessed September 2008).

[17] Alianza por la Proteccion Laboral (2007) 'Situación de los derechos laborales y el acceso a la justicia de los hombres y mujeres que trabajan en la maquila', www.codemuh.org/index.php?option=com_content&task=view &id=22&Itemid=2 (last accessed September 2008).

[18] See also W. Macdonald (2008) 'Work-related musculoskeletal disorders in a globalising world', Collaborating Centre Connection, www.cdc.gov/niosh/ CCC/CCCnewsV1N5.html#d (last accessed September 2008).

[19] National Research Council and C. Rigby (2004) *Monitoring International Labor Standards: International Perspectives – Summary of Regional Forums*, Washington DC: National Academies Press.

[20] Centro de Derechos de Mujeres (2007) 'Violacion de las garantias constitucionales de libertad de peticion y asociacion : represion y listas negras en las empresas maquiladoras de Honduras', San Pedro Sula, www.derechosdelamujer.org/html/PUBLICACIONES/lista%20negra.pdf (last accessed September 2008).

[21] Make Trade Fair (n.d.) 'Honduras: Campaign for Labour Protection', www.maketradefair.com/en/index.php?file=06022004160816.htm (last accessed September 2008).

[22] National Research Council and C. Rigby (2004), *op.cit.*, p. 21.

[23] Make Trade Fair (n.d.), *op.cit.*

[24] B. Torres and A. L. Restrepo (2006) 'Systematization of CODEMUH's experience on advocacy and lobby work on labor rights and occupational health 2002–2005', Oxfam GB.

[25] D. Dalton (2007) *Building National Campaigns*, Oxford: Oxfam, http://publications.oxfam.org.uk/oxfam/display.asp?K=9780855985745&sf_2 0=oxfam_archive_flag&st_20=NOT+Y&sf_01=CTITLE&st_01=building+natio nal+campaigns&sort=SORT_DATE%2FD&m=2&dc=2 (last accessed September 2008).

[26] B. Torres and A. L. Restrepo (2006), *op.cit.*

[27] *La Tribuna* (2007) 'Enfermedades respiratorias estan acabando con obreras de las maquilas', Tegucigalpa, 24 de Enero, www.latribuna.hn/news/45/ARTICLE/3841/2007-01-24.html (last accessed September 2008).

[28] Red de Desarrollo Sostenible (2008) 'Mujeres plantean reformas', http://listas.rds.hn/movimiento-popular/msg01595.html (last accessed September 2008).

[29] Tiempo Digital (2006) 'Empleadas de maquilas comienzan a ser escuchadas', 30 de septiembre, www.tiempo.hn/mostrar_noticia.php ?id=10238&seccion=1 (last accessed September 2008).

[30] Interview with Jorge Romero, radio station manager quoted by B. Torres and A. L. Restrepo (2006), *op.cit.*

[31] B. Torres and A. L. Restrepo (2006), *op.cit.*

[32] Interview with Maria Luisa Regalado, CODEMUH's co-ordinator, quoted by B. Torres and A. L. Restrepo (2006), *op.cit.*

Cover photo: Dunia Perez/CODEMUH (1 May 2008)

© Oxfam GB, November 2008

This paper was written by Juan-Carlos Arita. We acknowledge the assistance of Tania Garcia, Asier Hernando Malax-Echevarria, and Ariel Torres in its production. Thank you to Nikki van der Gaag who edited the paper and to Emily Laurie who provided research assistance. It is part of a series of papers written to inform public debate on development and humanitarian policy issues. The text may be freely used for the purposes of campaigning, education, and research, provided that the source is acknowledged in full.

For further information please email publish@oxfam.co.uk

Online ISBN 978-1-84814-057-8. This paper is part of a set **Speaking Out: How the voices of poor people are shaping the future** available for purchase from Oxfam Publishing or its agents, print ISBN 978-0-85598-638-4 for the set of 12 papers. For more information visit http://publications.oxfam.org.uk/oxfam/display.asp?ISBN=9780855986384

This paper is also available in French and Spanish.

Oxfam GB

Oxfam GB is a development, relief, and campaigning organisation that works with others to find lasting solutions to poverty and suffering around the world. Oxfam GB is a member of Oxfam International.

Oxfam House
John Smith Drive
Cowley
Oxford
OX4 2JY

Tel: +44.(0)1865.473727
E-mail: enquiries@oxfam.org.uk
www.oxfam.org.uk

3. Building for the Future

Fostering local accountability in Malawi

Communities mobilise to demand their right to health care on World Health Day, organised by the Malawi Health Equity Network. The Malawi Economic Justice Network was one of the partners involved in the day.

President Hastings Banda held office in Malawi from 1964 to 1994. He discouraged any kind of participation in political decision-making, often under pain of death or imprisonment. Today, 15 years later, people in Malawi are still afraid to speak out. They do not have the experience or the structures to engage effectively in local advocacy work. This paper shows how the Catholic Commission for Justice and Peace (CCJP), supported by Oxfam, set about building confidence and economic literacy in local communities. Through learning about budget monitoring, ordinary men and women were able to begin to engage with those in power in order to improve their communities. If elections happen as proposed in 2009, these people will be in a good position to bring about real change on the ground.

Introduction

Malawi is a poor country. It ranks 164th out of 177 countries in the United Nations Human Development Index. Adult literacy between 1995 and 2005 was 64 per cent. Between 1990 and 2005, 20.8 per cent of people lived on less than $1 a day and 62.9 per cent on less than $2 a day.

From 1964, when Malawi gained its independence from the British, until 1994, when President Hastings Banda was ousted by a referendum, the country was a one-party state. Although President Banda came to power after defeating other parties, in 1971 he imposed a one-party system in Parliament, using his Malawi Congress Party majority. The constitution was then amended to recognise only one party, and he was made President for life.

President Banda not only banned other political parties, he discouraged and punished dissent or any form of political participation. People who tried to voice their opinions were punished through detention without trial, forfeiture of property, or exile.[1] Many chose to be passive as one way of keeping out of political trouble.

In May 1994, there was a general election which saw Banda being ousted and a new president, Bakili Muluzi, elected. The new constitution provided for democratic governance and limited presidential terms of office to five years. It also enshrined the rights of every individual to be heard. The 1994 general elections were followed with others in 1999 and 2004.

In 1998, a decentralisation policy enhanced local governance and gave local government more power. Local councillors were made accountable for prioritising development initiatives in the wards they represented, and for ensuring that resources channelled to local government were used appropriately.

However, the decentralisation policy was never fully applied, because local elections were not held as expected in 2004. There were many theories but no official explanation for this. Since then, Malawi has had no local councillors.[2] This has had an impact on the development of local democracy and on people's participation, as there are effectively no local representatives for decisions made at local level.

The Economic Literacy project

Recent studies have shown that it is still not easy for poor and vulnerable communities in Malawi to demand their rights.[3] They have little experience in speaking out and lack the knowledge and the confidence to know how to bring about change. It was for this reason that the Catholic Commission for Justice and Peace in Malawi (CCJP), and the Malawi Economic Justice Network (MEJN), with Oxfam providing financial and technical support, set up the Economic Literacy project, which ran between 2005 and 2007.[4]

The Catholic Commission for Justice and Peace (CCJP) and the Malawi Economic Justice Network (MEJN)

The Catholic Commission for Justice and Peace (CCJP) was established in 1996. The objective of the Commission is to create awareness and knowledge on social justice and human-rights issues in order to provide a breeding ground for integrated development and peace in the country. For example, CCJP has recently translated the Malawian Constitution into two local languages, and educated local trainers who distribute the constitution in villages and educate communities on human rights. CCJP also focuses on creating networks with the government and other organisations working to improve justice, human rights, democracy, and good governance.[5]

The Malawi Economic Justice Network (MEJN) is a coalition of more than 100 civil-society organisations with activities in the field of economic governance. MEJN's membership includes non-government organisations, community-based organisations, trade unions, representatives of the media, and academics, among others.[6]

MEJN worked on the project at national level, carrying out budget analysis and expenditure tracking and organising meetings with civil society to lobby MPs on specific commitments. CCJP worked locally to empower communities with the relevant knowledge and skills to hold their local councils accountable for their budgets.

The idea was to promote participation in order to enhance accountability and foster economic literacy, which would then lead to more active participation. People would then have the confidence to be able to demand their rights for the provision of basic social services such as water, or medical care, at local assembly and other levels, in the absence of local councillors.

MEJN would promote broad demands for health, education, and agriculture, for example, at national level, while CCJP would ensure that local communities were able to make similar demands at local level in three districts. CCJP built on the work it had already undertaken with the communities in these districts. It was important that trust had already been established and the groundwork done. CCJP was able to work both with formally recognised government structures and informal social networks. Through their structures, and in consultation with the district assembly, they identified the target communities where the project was to be carried out.

How the project worked

The project involved the participation of local people right from the design and planning stages. Gender, HIV, and AIDS were themes that ran through the whole project. There were three main stages:

1 A survey of social-service delivery in three districts

2 Consultation with opinion leaders and district executive committees

3 Organising communities for action

A survey of social-service delivery

Before the project began, CCJP carried out a social survey[7] of the areas where the project was intending to work, including Mayaka, Liwonde, Mlombozi, St. Lwanga in Zomba, Zomba Cathedral, Malemia, and Magomero. This was to assess the different social groupings in the survey area, identify which villages should be prioritised, and provide a map of the social services that people were currently using.

In the survey, communities raised a number of key concerns affecting their participation in society. These included the negative impact that HIV and AIDS had on many households; gender injustice, such as violence against women, due to deeply held cultural beliefs; and access to essential services such as water, health, and education. In addition, participants talked about the non-responsiveness of leaders and local government staff, and the dysfunctional state of local government structures resulting from the fact that local elections had not taken place in 2004.[8]

Ideas from the consultations on economic literacy

The consultations identified a range of problems and needs including access to drinking water, a health clinic, roads and bridges, schools, teachers and teaching aids, electricity, an irrigation scheme, market sanitation and security, and loans.

'We feel the national budget has nothing to do with us. We do not see how it benefits us. We have lost interest because we do not see the benefits trickle down to us', said village headman John Allabi Msosa who wants the government to build a school in his area and a bridge over the river on the Msosa–Mapanje road.

'We are thankful that CCJP has opened our minds. We now have an idea how we can get our needs to the attention of government through existing structures. Now we can meet and discuss development. We can discuss at village level, area level, traditional authority level, and then the assembly. In the absence of councillors, we know what to do', said senior group village head Mwembele.

For people from Jali, life would have been more bearable were schools built at Kholomana, Likoko, Jalitu, and Lamiteje, where pupils currently have to travel a long distance to go to school in Musheka. 'The result has been that the youngest of pupils have been disadvantaged. They either cannot make it to the school on foot or get there when classes are halfway through. In Mwambo, the classroom blocks are inadequate.'

'We also require a toilet at Jali market, a health clinic at Mpasa and at least one more ambulance', Hilda Kalinde, a hospital ward attendant, said.

At Magomero, unemployment, drinking water, access roads, and bridges came top on their needs list. 'Our children have problems when it rains as the bridge is in bad shape.'

Participants in Liwonde talked about health clinics being needed in Naungu, Kalonjele, and Nlyiwo; school blocks at Liwamba, Naungu, and Mombe; and boreholes at Kumbani, Nliwo, and Naungu, where people travel 20km to the nearest source of drinking water.

CCJP Economic Literacy Project Newsletter, February 2007, from and article by Gabriel Kamlomo

Consultation with leaders and district executive committees

The next stage consisted of a consultative process that brought together key opinion leaders including chiefs, religious leaders, and other leaders. Through a series of trainings, they were taken through basic concepts of budgeting at family level, and the importance of participating in local assembly budgets.[9]

Organising communities for action

CCJP facilitated a process of mobilising communities to ensure that as many people as possible were participating. This was mainly done through village discussion groups. From the initial stages, the targeted communities were involved in prioritising and shaping the project. A typical discussion group comprised 10–15 households (40–100 people). Each group had a small steering committee, which was responsible for collating issues and following them up in liaison with the CCJP co-ordinators.[10] The steering committees, which had up to ten members, were comprised of equal numbers of men and women.

Each steering committee was trained for three weeks, using participatory methodologies, in the basics of economic literacy and how budgets work.[11] This meant that over the period of the project there were increasing numbers of people in the communities willing to add their voices on issues affecting them, such as lack of support to orphans and vulnerable children, or the unavailability of health workers.[12]

Changing minds through economic literacy lessons

The gathering on this humid February Thursday did not appear unlike any other at Mayaka Catholic Parish grounds in Zomba save for the fact that this group of 84 men and women drawn from different religious denominations, the business community, and traditional leaders sitting under a tree shed had come on a unique mission: an Economic Literacy class.

Members of the gathering raise hands and periodically take to their feet to contribute to a discussion on how a family would ensure the availability, all year round, of its everyday needs such as food, shelter, and clothes. During such discussions, the participants, largely people with low levels of literacy, get enlightened on issues of economic rights, governance, and justice.

For example, Magret Chidima, 36, of Mlima village in traditional authority Malemia at Domasi in Zomba, had no idea that the money government announces as national budget included her own monetary contributions until this Thursday. 'I could hardly connect the tablet of soap that I buy every day for home use to the national budget. I am actually amazed to learn that the roads and bridges are built using our own money', said Chidima.

'With this project, we want to build the capacity of rural communities...to promote socio-economic justice. CCJP is trying to make people see the importance of taking part and influencing budgeting at family, community, and national levels', said CCJP Co-ordinator for Zomba Diocese, Clemence Alfazema.

CCJP Economic Literacy Project Newsletter, February 2007, from an article by Gabriel Kamlomo

In the course of the project, community representatives made a number of visits to their district assemblies to follow up on issues, and to put forward their demands. They also began monitoring development activities in their respective areas, and made quarterly reports in the local language. As a result of increasing community confidence, communities in the project areas were able to take traditional leaders to task over allegations of corruption, for example, during the distribution of fertiliser coupons.[13,14] Issues of bias in allocating district assembly resources were also raised.

Mainstreaming gender, HIV, and AIDS

In carrying out the project, efforts were made to see how lack of access to basic services affected men and women differently, with a view to addressing any gender challenges that women faced.[15]

CCJP felt that participation could not be complete and effective if women, who make up the majority of the population in the rural areas, were left out. CCJP undertook training on gender and put theory into practice by inviting equal numbers of men and women to the various trainings. This built on previous workshops on gender justice and human rights, which meant that there was less opposition than there might otherwise have been. Gender guidelines were drawn up by the community groups to ensure equality – for example, if the chairperson was a man, the deputy would be a woman.

Over the course of the project, women became more confident in speaking out, and some even had leadership roles. There was also a change in attitude towards women's voice and participation. Changing perceptions and gender attitudes is not an easy or a short intervention. It requires sustained efforts over a period of time. In a small way, however, this project started a process to show that both women and men have the right to speak out on issues affecting them.

Another issue on which CCJP felt it was important to train, in the context of economic literacy, was HIV and AIDS. In Malawi, more than 14.4 per cent of people aged 15 to 49 are infected with HIV.

Those who fall ill or die are often the most productive members of the community. The Economic Literacy project therefore included a session on the impact of HIV and AIDS on the community, in which participants are taught how an individual's illness would affect the economic welfare of a single home or family, the community they live in, and eventually the country.[16] 'When someone is taken ill, people tend to dedicate most of their time to caring for that person. That way, work in the field suffers. Eventually, a family's yearly incomes are negatively affected. People will need money for drugs for the patient, travel to places for medical help', explained Yusuf Stefano of Namahiya village in Chikowi traditional authority.

Successes, challenges, and lessons learned

The fact that local elections had not been held and that there were no local councillors was a big challenge for the project. It meant that in order to work on local budget accountability there also had to be a parallel focus on advocacy work, trying to get the national government to reinstate councillors at local government level and to put in place village development committees. Despite this challenge, the project succeeded in motivating ordinary citizens to participate and exercise their right to be heard on local budgets.

The project achieved two key successes:

- CCJP is now working on advocacy to ensure that local elections take place in 2009. The project built a good foundation for this work to take place. The fact that CCJP had already worked with and mobilised the target communities beforehand meant that it was not difficult to engage with these communities, since initial contacts and ways of working had been established.

- As a result of the project, many communities were able demand their rights and take local authorities to task. For example, initially, district assembly officials were reluctant to meet up with community representatives. Over time, however, and through a number of interactive meetings, there was more dialogue, and power relationships tipped in favour of the targeted communities. Local bureaucrats received delegations, and even visited local communities. The project also enhanced general participation, and allowed people confidently to voice their concerns about resource allocation to the local assembly administration.

One of the factors that helped achieve some of these successes was the fact that CCJP co-ordinators in the field used participatory methodologies in interacting with communities. Participation was therefore built into the project from the start. The surveys helped to unearth underlying factors impeding people's participation, such as lack of local government structures, gender biases, and the need for sustained facilitation and provision of knowledge – such as education on health rights, democracy, and HIV and AIDS – as well as skills to communities. These, and peoples' interest, led to increasing consciousness about basic entitlement to social-economic rights such as water and health.[17]

Village communities in Malawi have lots of energy and know what issues are most important for them. What they lack are the mechanisms to engage effectively with local government and hold their representatives accountable. Despite experiencing some constraints, the project managed to build capacity for advocacy, especially on economic justice issues. It promoted the mobilisation of communities around common issues in the targeted areas. And it began a process of empowering communities to enable them to participate and demand accountability from local authorities. When the elections do finally happen, hopefully in 2009, local people will be in a good position to know how to carry out effective advocacy work with the newly elected representatives.

Notes

[1] There were a number of laws such as the Forfeiture Act, Penal Code, and others which were used to punish those who opposed President Banda. It should be noted that most of these were amended when Malawi adopted a multi-party system of government and put in place a new constitution in 1994. The 1994 constitution established the National Compensation Tribunal to compensate victims of the one-party rule.

[2] The constitution requires that local government elections should be held every five years in accordance with the Local Government Act, 1998.

[3] For instance, the 'Malawi Annual Human Rights Report' (2006) and 'Human Rights Needs Assessment' (2004), Malawi Human Rights Resources Centre.

[4] This rationale was based on CCJP's own experience in working with rural communities in Malawi generally, but also in the areas where the project was implemented. CCJP included this reason as part of the background and justification for their interventions.

[5] Catholic Commission for Justice and Peace, www.ccjp-lilongwe.org; DanChurchAid Malawi 'Human Rights Organisations in Malawi', www.danchurchaid.org/sider_paa_hjemmesiden/where_we_work/africa/mal awi__1/read_more/human_rights_organisations_in_malawi (last accessed September 2008).

[6] Malawi Economic Justice Network, www.mejn.mw/ (last accessed September 2008).

[7] CCJP (2006) 'Progress Report', April.

[8] CCJP completed another survey in January 2008 where this issue also came out clearly.

[9] CCJP (2005) 'Project document'.

[10] This information comes from project visits and progress project reports from CCJP.

[11] CCJP (2006), *op.cit.*

[12] *Ibid.*

[13] *Ibid.*

[14] See for instance the Ministry of Agriculture's 'Input Subsidy Programme 2007/08'.

[15] Several studies have documented the fact that women face more gender injustices than men. See for example WILSA (Malawi) (2000) *In Search of Justice: Women and Administration of Justice in Malawi,* Blantyre: Dzuka Publishing Company.

[16] *Ibid.*

[17] See sections 25 and 30 of the Malawi constitution, respectively.

Cover photograph: Ben Matemba, Health Rights Initiative (April 2008)

© Oxfam GB, November 2008

This paper was written by Shenard Mazengera. We acknowledge the assistance of CCJP in its production. Thank you to Nikki van der Gaag who edited the paper and to Emily Laurie who provided research assistance. It is part of a series of papers written to inform public debate on development and humanitarian policy issues. The text may be freely used for the purposes of campaigning, education, and research, provided that the source is acknowledged in full.

For further information please email publish@oxfam.co.uk

Online ISBN 978-1-84814-058-5. This paper is part of a set **Speaking Out: How the voices of poor people are shaping the future** available for purchase from Oxfam Publishing or its agents, print ISBN 978-0-85598-638-4 for the set of 12 papers. For more information visit http://publications.oxfam.org.uk/oxfam/display.asp?ISBN=9780855986384

This paper is also available in French and Spanish.

Oxfam GB

Oxfam GB is a development, relief, and campaigning organisation that works with others to find lasting solutions to poverty and suffering around the world. Oxfam GB is a member of Oxfam International.

Oxfam House
John Smith Drive
Cowley
Oxford
OX4 2JY

Tel: +44.(0)1865.473727
E-mail: enquiries@oxfam.org.uk
www.oxfam.org.uk

Programme Insights

4. Tackling Corruption

Lessons from Oxfam's work

Electoral Observation Mission Peace Week March, Sincelejo, Colombia

Corruption drives poverty, powerlessness, and exclusion in societies where having little cash or influence means no access to basic entitlements, public services, justice, or even physical security. But corruption is not an isolated issue. It is part of a set of societal, economic, political, and cultural systems that deny people in poverty access to rights and resources. For this reason, Oxfam sees work on corruption as integral to rights-based work which seeks to increase the power of people in poverty to demand change, and the accountability and capacity of governments to deliver it. This paper examines Oxfam's approach to corruption and its work in several different countries. It also outlines key corruption issues for those working in development.

Introduction

Why is corruption an important issue for development? Corruption causes poverty and constrains poverty reduction. In societies where having little cash or influence means no access to public services, basic entitlements, or even physical security, corruption drives poverty, powerlessness, and exclusion by diverting scarce resources intended to improve poor people's lives.

What is corruption? A variety of definitions exist, but Oxfam defines it as 'the abuse of entrusted power for private gain'. Corruption diverts public resources away from social sectors and poor people, increasing the cost of public services, lowering their quality, and often restricting access to such essential services as water, health, and education. Corruption also limits the development and economic growth of a country, and perpetuates the unequal distribution of power, wealth, and resources. While corruption impacts negatively on most segments of society, people living in poverty lack the economic, social, and political power necessary to challenge corrupt practices and are more vulnerable than most to extortion, bribery, double standards, and intimidation.

So how does corruption affect the right to be heard? It is not just about financial loss; it is about control of, access to, and distribution of, resources in society. It cannot be isolated from broader governance problems where governments and the powerful operate with impunity and people lack the power to challenge them. The absence of corruption, therefore, is a key part of good governance. Corruption makes it harder to influence decision-makers and empower poor people, and works against their right to be heard.

Who is most affected? As usual, those with the fewest resources and least power are the hardest hit. Women living in poverty, for example, are vulnerable to sexual exploitation with little power to challenge abusers, and excluded from the basic services they need in their caring roles.

These are issues that concern non-government organisations (NGOs) every day, whether they are working on livelihoods, emergency relief, or human rights. Development organisations have a responsibility to their supporters and beneficiaries to ensure that aid is used as effectively as possible – both protecting their own resources and playing a part in monitoring the effective use of government investments in anti-poverty programmes. They also need to practise what they preach and remain free of corruption themselves, both as a model and in order to ensure a relationship of trust with their partners.

What is Oxfam's approach to corruption?

Oxfam takes a rights-based approach to its development, humanitarian, and campaigning work. This means we recognise that imbalances in power relations prevent people in poverty from exercising their rights; that much of our work is participatory; and that all development actors and all stakeholders are accountable to one another.

Oxfam GB recently undertook an internal review of its programme and policy on corruption work, which included a global survey of the experience and opinions of over 80 staff and partners across 30 countries. The results are of interest to other international NGOs reviewing their approach to such work.

Staff and partners surveyed by Oxfam made it clear that corruption is not an isolated or stand-alone issue – it is part of a set of societal, economic, political, and cultural systems that deny people in poverty access to rights and resources. Many staff emphasised the importance of starting with the problems facing people in poverty. For people with no access to medical care or schools for their children, it makes little difference whether the cause is corruption, weak public policy, or lack of resources.

For this reason Oxfam sees work on corruption as part of a range of work to increase the power of people in poverty to demand change, and the accountability and capacity of governments to deliver it. It is therefore central to the theme of the right to be heard.

This paper gives a number of examples of campaigns and organisations successfully fighting corruption. They were chosen because they were areas where Oxfam has programme experience on or around the issue of corruption, and because they agreed to participate in the research. These include monitoring campaign financing in Chile; monitoring elections in Colombia; and tracking public spending in Malawi and Indonesia. From these examples and others, a number of lessons for supporting future programme work on corruption are outlined.

Oxfam's work on corruption

Oxfam GB funds a range of development work on corruption. Most is indirect, and focuses on improving accountability and the participation of people in poverty in decisions which affect their lives, as a contribution to creating an environment where corruption is less likely to flourish. Much of this consists of participatory budget work and budget analysis; participation of communities in public decision-making; and campaigning for public accountability and corporate social responsibility. For example:

- Funding anti-corruption organisations in Uganda, Cambodia, and Indonesia.

- Supporting work on political reforms and election monitoring in Chile and Colombia.

- Holding business to account through the Extractive Industries Transparency Initiative (EITI). The EITI is a coalition of governments, companies, civil-society groups, investors, and international organisations. It supports improved governance in resource-rich countries through the verification and full publication of company payments and government revenues from oil, gas, and mining.

- A Publish What You Pay (PWYP) campaign in West Africa and Bolivia. The PWYP is a coalition of over 300 NGOs worldwide which calls for the mandatory disclosure of the payments made by oil, gas, and mining companies to all governments for the extraction of natural resources.

- Some engagement with multilateral anti-corruption initiatives such as the UN Convention Against Corruption (UNCAC). Adopted in October 2003, the UNCAC creates the opportunity to develop a global language about corruption and a coherent implementation strategy. It is a multilateral legal and international co-operation mechanism against corruption, signed by over 200 countries. It requires states to take action on private-sector corruption and to improve the integrity and accountability of public affairs. There is a 'friends of the UNCAC' coalition of NGOs from 40 countries, using the UNCAC as an important platform for national and international work on corruption. A multitude of international anti-corruption agreements exist, but their implementation has been uneven and only moderately successful. The UNCAC gives the global community the opportunity to address both of these weaknesses and begin establishing an effective set of benchmarks for effective anti-corruption strategies. The Global Programme against Corruption (GPAC) is a catalyst and a resource to help countries effectively implement the provision of the UNCAC.

In its humanitarian response, Oxfam works to make vulnerable people aware of their entitlements and rights; as part of this we aim to prevent people being coerced into financial, sexual, or other favours in return for food, shelter, and so on. For several years, Oxfam GB has been part of various inter-agency initiatives to improve accountability to people affected by disasters, including participating in a peer-review process to improve accountability in its own work and that of others in the sector. Oxfam also works on the prevention of abuse and exploitation of beneficiaries by international and national relief and development workers by training staff, informing affected communities of their rights and entitlements, and working to ensure that complaints mechanisms are in place, functional, and accessible to all.

The political process, elections, and financing

Much of Oxfam's corruption work is based on improving the relationship between people in poverty and governments; empowering citizens to demand more from governments, and supporting governments and others in power to deliver their responsibilities to citizens. It is crucial to work with both people in poverty and people in power in order to bring about real change.

In Chile, Colombia, and Indonesia, Oxfam and its partners believe that work on corruption should start at the root cause: political culture, which is seen to 'infect' the rest of society. This means taking every opportunity to tackle corruption at key points such as elections, corruption scandals, changes in legislation, and parliamentary reforms.

'We need a change of political and state culture – if you are a Minister you have to believe that you are a public servant and you fulfil the law and respond to the public. This idea is obvious to us, for the [politicians] it's an idea from another planet', says an Oxfam partner in Chile.

Countering corruption in Colombia: monitoring elections

More than 40 years of conflict in Colombia have created a state where many areas are dominated by powerful interest groups, who have benefited from a weakened rule of law, and a democratic and accountability deficiency in local institutions. For example, a recent police investigation exposed a plot by paramilitary leaders to fund electoral candidates in local elections, in return for a reward from public expenditure on social services.

In this context, monitoring elections becomes very important. In the 2006 elections, more than 60 per cent of the electorate stayed away and more than a million people spoiled their ballots. In October 2007, Oxfam GB supported the Electoral Observation Mission (MOE) to monitor the mayoral and regional elections in districts most affected by violence and conflict. The findings provide a window onto the whole electoral monitoring process, which is seen as an important way of protecting candidates. According to the MOE, there was illegal pressure on ordinary citizens in more than half the municipalities (576 of 1,099). The findings also demonstrated the substantial risk to the electoral candidates themselves. The MOE used the information on the candidates to create a map of electoral risk. The electoral monitoring process also provides valuable contextual analysis that helps to inform Oxfam GB's work on humanitarian and protection issues.

Case study from MOE

One of the ways of countering corruption is to push for access to information as a legally guaranteed right, as the following example of Oxfam GB's work in Chile shows. If people know what their rights are, they are more likely to be able to see when corruption is happening and perhaps do something about it.

Challenging collusion between politics and business in Chile

Two examples of Oxfam partners in Chile working on access to information on elections and public policy show the importance of such work in improving transparency, reducing corruption, and allowing ordinary citizens to make a difference.

Monitoring elections and campaign financing

PARTICIPA, an NGO and Oxfam partner, started as a campaign to peacefully vote Pinochet out of office in 1987. Seven thousand volunteers around the country encouraged people to vote in a referendum and conducted political education with voters, a key influence on the peaceful expulsion of Pinochet from office. Since then PARTICIPA has continued to push for constitutional amendments to improve the functioning of elections, to improve electoral participation, to bring citizens into public decision-making, and to increase transparency in public policy. In 2002, PARTICIPA used new laws on electoral spending to monitor the spending of over 80 parliamentary candidates. The results, along with related corruption scandals, shocked the public and angered politicians, resulting in the tabling of a new law and greater regulatory oversight on campaign financing.

Access to information as a powerful campaign tool

TERRAM is an environmental organisation working on social and economic issues. It meets with government and parliamentarians as a non-profit lobby, does lots of public-information work, participates in law proposals, and writes articles on key reform agendas. TERRAM successfully brought the first legal action against a government body (*Corporación Nacional Forestal*, CONAF – the National Forestry Commission) for access to public information using the new probity law, which contains regulations on public access. CONAF was found guilty on all counts and compelled to provide information and cover legal costs. This was a groundbreaking case leading to a number of advancements in transparency and probity in public office.

Corruption in non-formal power structures excludes women

The use and abuse of informal power is a significant source of corruption in many countries. It can particularly affect women's access to power and resources. Oxfam partners in East Africa and Indonesia point to traditional leadership structures that exclude women from decision-making:

'Right now there is powerful competition between elites and interest groups – this prevents the needs of women and the poor to be taken up to higher level. On top of this women's access to decision-making is limited by patriarchal culture; they are subordinated and criticised if they are outside the house too much', says a member of the Institute of Community Justice, an Oxfam partner in Indonesia.

Supporting women's voices, increasing their power, and improving accountability within informal structures is a long process. NGOs can help by maintaining good contact with government and advocating for women's participation in all decision-making structures. At community level, women need to be aware that they are important, and their voices and aspirations count as much as men's. Gaining the support and political will of local and traditional leaders is also crucial.

The importance of a strong community presence

'We used to do the [budget] analysis ourselves, do the lobbying and file court cases. But the legal process is not effective and at the same time we were not building awareness among the public. Ordinary people give a lot of weight to other people's official status – this generates a climate in which corruption becomes acceptable. So building awareness in communities is very important', says an Oxfam partner in Indonesia.

Many organisations funded by Oxfam highlight the importance of community work in combating corruption. It is seen as essential to building the voice of people in poverty, raising awareness about rights, challenging tolerance of corruption, and creating the demand for higher standards from public office. A strong community presence is also key to the legitimacy and credibility of organisations working on corruption, as the examples below show.

Monitoring public spending in Malawi's schools

The Civil Society Coalition for Quality Basic Education (CSCQBE) is a coalition of NGOs, community groups, community service organisations, and education networks working together to improve public education policy in Malawi. Every year since 2001, the coalition has surveyed the public education budget, and supported school committees, parent–teacher associations, and community organisations to monitor public spending in schools. The coalition publishes its findings, conducts lobby meetings with government and donors, and feeds into parliamentary hearings.

Their work has exposed a number of problems including the financing of 'ghost' teachers (who appear on the salary roll but never turn up) and schools, and the charging of administration fees by regional governments for handling school funds. It has contributed indirectly to the prosecution of the former Education Minister for spending public funds on his wedding.

CSCQBE's constant pressure and surveillance has done much to open up the Malawian government to civil-society demands for greater accountability:

'The budget monitoring exercise has added a voice for Malawian civil society in demanding social services and accountability. CSCQBE has become a force to reckon with, and the government is forced to make statements and clarify what it is doing with public resources', says Limbani Nsapato, CSCQBE's Director.

Based on conversation with Limbani Nsapato, Director of CSCQBE and L. Nsapato (2005) 'Budget Monitoring: Survey of Education Expenditures in Malawi', CSCQBE.

Social sanctions for corrupt behaviour in Kupang, West Timor, Indonesia

The Initiative for the Development of People's Advocacy (PIAR) has been investigating and publicising corruption in West Timor since 1996. It analyses and investigates the use of province budgets; helps district governments improve their planning and respond better to communities; and educates community members about their rights. One of the ways this is done is through Participatory Poverty Assessments, which gather information from people in poverty in order to provide the necessary information to address local needs.

Since working with Oxfam, PIAR have changed their approach from a purely investigative, confrontational role with government, to an approach that is more collaborative and takes a more constructive approach with the district, city, and province authorities. They have had a number of successes. PIAR campaigned for the repeal of a law which permitted MPs in Kupang to vote themselves a pay rise at twice the legal limit. PIAR Director Sarah Lery Mboeik feels their success has given them the clout needed to press for other improvements: 'We felt proud because corruption by politicians became a big issue in province, this gives us a better bargaining position with the government – they're scared of us now.'

Working with governments and the private sector to deliver accountability

Making accountability work takes more than upward pressure on government from civil society. Working with governments themselves is also crucial if there is to be an improvement in their responsiveness to citizens and their capacity to deliver on public services. Oxfam partners such as KOPAL (an Indonesian organisation founded in 2000 by journalists and university students, whose vision is for MPs to be more accountable and responsive to their constituents) train MPs on budget law and how to respond to constituents. KOPAL also monitors them against a code of conduct and creates 'political contracts' between politicians and their constituents, by organising regular public meetings where politicians discuss their progress against their campaign promises.

'It's crucial that the legislature functions efficiently and accountably – but it is also crucial that communities are critical of the legislature and public policy functions. As voters, they need to be aware of why they are participating, who they are voting for, and whether that candidate is responding to their interests and needs', says KOPAL's director, Sam Suddin.

Working in alliance with other organisations

Working with like-minded organisations on corruption is crucial in order to share ideas and approaches, increase influence, and provide 'safety in numbers'. Strong protests from NGO allies prevented the expulsion of anti-corruption NGOs in a number of countries. For example, a decision to bar a Philippine anti-corruption NGO from the international UNCAC conference was reversed after protests by a global coalition of NGOs in December 2006.

International NGOs need to use their voices to campaign for multilateral mechanisms against corruption; to pressurise multinationals and national companies to act accountably; and to support the work of national anti-corruption organisations such as UNCAC, EITI, and PWYP.

NGOs as role models

Attitudes and beliefs about the acceptable use of power in society are critical, and an obvious entry point for NGOs. Oxfam staff point to the fact that cultural practices in many societies legitimise forms of nepotism, with the use of influence to assist family and community seen as normal, and part of a coping strategy for people in poverty. This has implications for NGOs too: there are inevitably pressures on staff members to use their position to benefit family and community. It is important to emphasise that corruption is not a moral or cultural problem exclusive to developing countries, as recent corruption scandals in the West illustrate.

'There's social acceptance of some kinds of corruption: no-one's hurt, you've managed to help yourself and your people. The thought that these practices are unfair and limit the resources available to others is not appreciated', says an Oxfam staff member from the Horn, East, and Central Africa Region.

This is a key issue: NGOs should be role models of non-corrupt institutions, particularly where traditions and customs of kinship and collective support can undermine more general notions of solidarity and meritocracy. In order to do this, staff will have to be open and brave enough to talk about and address corruption within their own organisations. This means working with staff to understand corruption within the local context; making sure that programme work is free of corruption; and being consistent and credible to beneficiaries.

In terms of internal integrity, Oxfam GB is committed to high legal, ethical, and moral standards in all its work, and supports this through codes of conduct, its internal policies, and the work of its dedicated loss-prevention team. Oxfam GB's internal Code of Conduct requires all staff to adhere to high standards of professionalism and integrity in keeping with Oxfam's beliefs, values, and aims. Oxfam GB has an internal Anti-Fraud and Corruption Guidance which sets out procedures to assist staff and managers in preventing, detecting, and handling fraud.

To improve Oxfam's accountability to its beneficiaries in humanitarian responses, Oxfam has been participating in a peer-review process with eight other international organisations. Progress in improving accountability to affected populations is being made in some places with simple actions on the ground, and has been shown to pay for itself, both in humanitarian and financial terms, as the case study below shows.

Accountability to food-aid recipients in Malawi

In 2005–2006 there was a food crisis in Southern Africa. More than 12 million people were affected in seven countries. In Malawi, 35 per cent of the population was in dire need of food.[1] This resulted in a large-scale food-aid programme, the accountability of which was examined by Oxfam. An Oxfam humanitarian team surveyed 1,200 aid recipients through focus-group discussions and 'pocket voting', which allows communities to voice their opinions through a visual feedback form. The people choose a face, which shows a certain emotion, to respond to questions.

Overall, 70 per cent of those surveyed rated themselves as 'happy' with the way they had been able to interact with Oxfam.[2] The evaluation team did not speak to a single person who was confused about entitlements, ignorant of the fact that humanitarian aid is free, or who had missed a distribution because they were confused or ill-informed. The team learned that beneficiaries had been able to report corruption and theft through mechanisms set up by Oxfam. For example, one community feared they were being defrauded by a man working in the transition of grain from the Oxfam suppliers to the people. Community members approached the police, who investigated, found the man guilty, and punished him appropriately. This was possible due to prior discussions between the community, partners, Malawian police, and Oxfam, all of whom had reached an agreement on how such incidents should be approached.

Case study from field pilots as part of the Humanitarian Accountability Proposal 2007 (unpublished) Yo Winder, Oxfam GB

Oxfam believes that work on anti-corruption should recognise the importance of:

- Improving how people use entrusted power – including private, public, and informal structures. Improving how governments use public resources is a priority, given their duty to drive development, protect human rights, and reduce poverty.

- Social attitudes towards corruption, the distribution of resources, and the way power is used.

- Action from developed countries' governments and companies to tackle the supply-side of corruption by improving corporate accountability and supporting multilateral initiatives against corruption.

Lessons learned

Oxfam has learned a number of lessons during the course of its work against corruption with partners in many different countries:

1 **Attitudes and beliefs** about the use of power and about accountability are an important entry point for NGOs into work on governance and corruption.

2 **The political process, elections, and financing** are key to fighting corruption – it is important to make the most of opportunities for change during these times.

3 It is crucial to **work at a number of levels** on corruption issues – both with people in poverty and with people in power; and at local, national, and international levels. It is also important to form alliances with other NGOs and anti-corruption networks as this increases influence and provides protection to NGOs in sensitive environments.

4 This is a **long-term project** – over and over again those working on corruption point out that this is not something that happens quickly and easily.

5 **NGOs are important** as role models of accountability and integrity. It is important to practise what you preach – trust once lost is not easily regained.

Notes

[1] British Red Cross (2006) 'Food for thousands of Malawi families', www.redcross.org.uk/news.asp?id=51572 (last accessed September 2008).

[2] 'Of the remaining 30%, 5% were neutral, 12% were sad, and 12% were angry'. From case study from field pilots as part of the Humanitarian Accountability Proposal 2007 (unpublished) Yo Winder, Oxfam GB.

Cover photograph: Misión de Observación Electoral, 9 September 2008

© Oxfam GB, November 2008

This paper was written by Bethan Emmett. Thank you to Nikki van der Gaag who edited the paper and to Emily Laurie who provided research assistance. It is part of a series of papers written to inform public debate on development and humanitarian policy issues. The text may be freely used for the purposes of campaigning, education, and research, provided that the source is acknowledged in full.

For further information please email: publish@oxfam.org.uk

Online ISBN 978-1-84814-059-2. This paper is part of a set **Speaking Out: How the voices of poor people are shaping the future** available for purchase from Oxfam Publishing or its agents, print ISBN 978-0-85598-638-4 for the set of 12 papers. For more information visit http://publications.oxfam.org.uk/oxfam/display.asp?ISBN=9780855986384

This paper is also available in French and Spanish.

Oxfam GB

Oxfam GB is a development, relief, and campaigning organisation that works with others to find lasting solutions to poverty and suffering around the world. Oxfam GB is a member of Oxfam International.

Oxfam House
John Smith Drive
Cowley
Oxford
OX4 2JY

Tel: +44.(0)1865.473727
E-mail: enquiries@oxfam.org.uk
www.oxfam.org.uk

5. Finding a Voice for the Voiceless

Indigenous people gain recognition in Bangladesh

Adibashi *children in the pre-primary education initiative*

Despite the fact that the government has signed international agreements protecting their rights, the 2.2 million indigenous or *adibashi* peoples of Bangladesh experience structural prejudice, discrimination, and violence from the majority Bengali community. They lack power and influence at community, regional, and national levels. In response to this, Oxfam GB and its 20 partner organisations set up the Indigenous People's Capacity Building Programme. This aimed to ensure that the northern *adibashi* peoples, who are the most discriminated against, could hold the government to account. The programme increased the numbers of *adibashi* children in primary school, improved women's participation in traditional social structures, helped *adibashis* claim land, and made them less vulnerable to exploitation. This has increased the community's confidence and helped them to speak out and claim their rights.

Introduction

Bangladesh has a total area of 143,998 square kilometres and a population of over 150 million, making it one of the most densely populated countries in the world. There are 45 different indigenous communities in Bangladesh, thought to comprise about 1.74 million people or approximately 1.2 per cent of the population (provisional census report 2001).[1] They are also known as *adivasi*, *adibashi*, or 'aboriginal people'. The government prefers the term 'tribals'. Levels of poverty and inequality are high. The country ranks 140th out of 177 countries in the Human Development Index,[2] with 41 per cent of the population living below the poverty line in 2000.

Vulnerability of adibashis

The *adibashis* are among the poorest people in the country and live mainly by subsistence agriculture. [3] They have their own traditions and customs, different from those of the mainstream culture. Despite the fact that the government has signed a number of international conventions[4] protecting their rights, indigenous peoples have yet to receive due recognition under the constitution of Bangladesh. The most disadvantaged groups live in the north-western plains, where in 1991, it was estimated that 85 per cent were landless and only 9 per cent were literate.[5] They face ethnic violence and poverty.

The government of Bangladesh has no *adibashi*-centred policies, or a single department to address their development issues. They are largely deprived of state services, have limited access to government resources, and lack representation in decision-making at the local or national levels.

There is also widespread prejudice against *adibashis* by the majority Bengali population, and a belief that they are not capable of learning. As a result, they are often excluded from national education plans; there is no provision for the Bangla-based curriculum to include their different languages, and the education system does not portray a positive image of their life and culture.

In addition, landowners often bribe the local land office to produce fake papers to favour landowners who have grabbed land from the *adibashis*, who tend not to own land as individuals but have inherited it from their ancestors.[6]

All this is made worse by the fact that the different *adibashi* groups do not have a united voice, nor access to the information they need to claim their rights.

The Indigenous People's Capacity Building Programme

A rights-based approach

Since independence in 1971, the national and local non-government organisation (NGO) sector in Bangladesh has largely developed as a service-delivery sector. Many NGOs are sub-contracted by international NGOs, donors, and sometimes government, to provide essential and basic services. Very few work with minority groups from a rights perspective.

In 2000, Oxfam GB initiated what was originally called the Indigenous People's Development Programme in north-west Bangladesh, with the aim of ensuring that the northern *adibashi* peoples were aware of their rights, empowered to claim them from the government, and that they would be recognised as equal with the majority Bengali community. Initial consultations involved four workshops plus discussions with community leaders and civil-society organisations at regional and national levels. The main outcome of this first stage was a list of priority issues, including: capacity-building of organisations; land rights; education; reducing violence against women; reducing social exclusion; and sustainable livelihoods. Following on from this, it was essential to ensure that local communities and Oxfam partner organisations were willing to take a rights-based approach. The programme then developed in phases as community members gradually gained experience in identifying problems and solutions themselves, and so began leading the process.

The programme expanded significantly in 2006 with the support of DANIDA,[7] adding 16 partner organisations in eight additional districts. Today, the programme has evolved into the Indigenous People's Capacity Building Progamme and a rights-based approach is well established. It consists of three main strands:

1   Building trust within communities

2   Building the capacity and leadership skills of women and men in grassroots organisations

3   Training community groups in human rights and advocacy.

The 19 partners have worked together to establish the rights of the community and create leadership; Oxfam and its partners now work only in a facilitation role.

This whole approach is breaking a trend in Bangladesh, where traditionally NGOs work in parallel with the government by providing the same services. Instead, this programme motivates *adibashi* people to claim what is theirs from the government. The programme binds the state duty-bearers (government officials) to fulfil their obligations towards the rights-holders (indigenous communities).

Through the programme, Oxfam has developed some entry points for the *adibashi* people to feel confident as a community and to improve their awareness of their rights and how to claim them. Most importantly, the *adibashis* know that they are no longer alone and that they are supported in their struggles to find a lasting solution to their complex problems.

Women's participation and leadership

Women's leadership has also been at the heart of the programme, which has aimed to give women the information, skills, and confidence to speak out about their own issues and to feel they have support in doing so. Women are no longer being ignored in the communities, as they are being included in traditionally male-dominated social structures: even though this is sometimes just as observers sitting in traditional governance forums (without decision-making powers), it is a far cry from the early days of the programme where the inclusion of women was unthinkable. As the programme develops in the future, women's leadership in decision-making processes will need to be further strengthened.

Pre-primary education

Low levels of education and literacy among the *adibashi* community have contributed to their lack of understanding about what rights they have, and the means by which to access them. Accordingly, education was one of the priority areas identified during the initial discussions in 2000. The programme has particularly focused on pre-primary education as a key entry point into the mainstream school system.

Bangladesh does not have an initiative or policy to educate *adibashi* children in their mother tongue or to portray the values, cultures, and traditions of *adibashis* properly in the national textbooks. The key obstacle for *adibashis* in accessing mainstream education include language, treatment by peers and teachers, the curriculum, context of textbooks, types of instruction, and remoteness of villages. *Adibashi* children are fluent in their own languages but are often weak in Bengali, the national language.

Oxfam partners brought together a group of education and programme strategy specialists along with community leaders and programme participants to plan how *adibashi* children could start to access education services. First, a one-year community-led pre-primary education programme was devised. Bilingual textbooks, sensitivity training for teachers and parents, and information sharing were tools used to assist the children. The aim was to reduce the language barrier, increase school attendance, and support the *adibashi* children in reaching the level required to participate fully in primary school and express their needs and opinions.

Second, school principals and head teachers were brought on board at an early stage. There was initial resistance from many head teachers due to a mixture of traditional prejudice, limited information, and fear that their school ratings might drop if lower-level students were admitted. However, the partners and community organisations promoted the use of the textbooks and encouraged head teachers to visit successful community programmes. This gradually resulted in an acceptance of, and confidence in, the programme.

As a result of the programme there are now 105 community organisations, some of which are pre-primary schools, all set up to build trust, increase attendance, and increase *adibashi* children's confidence. The fact these organisations are 'community-owned' has been very important to the programme's success. Previously, *adibashi* parents did not feel willing or able to send their children to primary schools, but now almost 100 per cent of school-age *adibashi* children in some areas are enrolled in the government primary education system. The primary-school attendance rate for *adibashi* children increased from 10 per cent four years ago to its current level of 98 per cent: some 1300 children. More than half of these are girls. 'The *adibashi* students are doing better than the Bengali students in class and we are very pleased with them. We will try to give more stipends and other facilities to the promising youngsters', said Ms Kamrunnessa, Joyenpur School Principal, in 2006.[8]

A major success of the programme was that the government's Department of Primary Education used the model developed by the programme to produce the first training manual for the civil servants who supervise the teachers working for the inclusion of indigenous children in education.

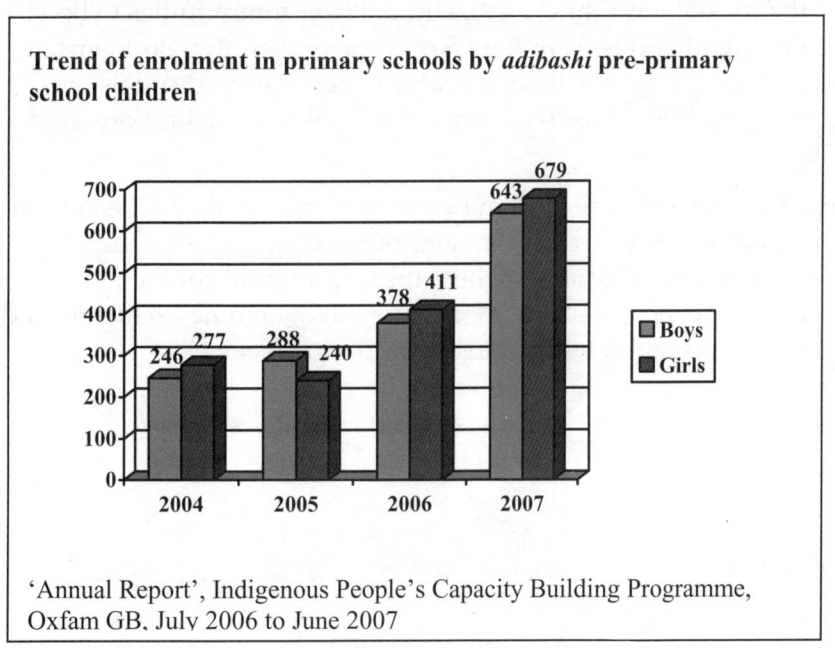

Trend of enrolment in primary schools by *adibashi* pre-primary school children

'Annual Report', Indigenous People's Capacity Building Programme, Oxfam GB, July 2006 to June 2007

Working with adults

In addition, the programme established forums for the mothers of the children attending pre-primary school to come together once a month and talk about and address issues of concern. These forums are largely supported by male members of the family because they see the positive impact on the family and community as a whole. Discussions are held on various topics to do with health, hygiene, sanitation, nutrition, and encouragement to continue sending their children to school.

One issue was that the *adibashi* children were suffering from a lack of nutrition which meant they could not engage actively in education. To reduce this, the mothers' forum organised regular cooking and distribution to the children of nutritious food. To acclimatise mothers (from the forum) and children to the new atmosphere and expose them to broader horizons, exchange visits were organised with other pre-primary schools. This further encouraged both mothers and children to make new friends and discuss issues, and built the women's confidence.

The programme also works with adults and young people via the Adibashi Bikash Kendra (Adibashi Development Centre) and the Human Resources Development Centre for adult and youth learning, which involve around 30 people. These initiatives cover literacy, action to reduce social conflicts, action against discrimination, protection against eviction, solving of small-scale problems, and the promotion of cultural practices.

Most of the *adibashi* communities have their own traditional social structures, but many of these had broken down in the face of discrimination. The programme is trying to reactivate these. So far, 135 traditional structures have been set up, with 169 women involved as observer participants. They meet once a month to discuss and solve their problems. These enable the *adibashi* communities to be more organised and feel empowered to solve their own problems. They promote *adibashi* distinctive culture, heritage, and rituals by organising traditional festivals, sports, special day celebrations, and so on.

In addition, *adibashis* are working to recover land grabbed illegally by landowners, to lobby for government-owned land (*khash* – see below), to practise mediation where there is internal conflict, to ensure social justice, to share information, to overcome exclusion, and to increase interaction with mainstream Bengali society.

Evolving into community-based organisations

Isolation from the mainstream Bengali community makes *adibashi* people vulnerable to prejudice and violence and threatens the survival of their culture. Oxfam and its partners seek to reduce social exclusion and ensure a better quality of life and security for *adibashis* through promoting better social organisation and inter-community relationships. To this end, they provide support to establish and strengthen community-based organisations that promote indigenous culture, language, heritage, and provide security.

With the facilitation of the partner organisations, the community-based organisations have had training on areas such as writing operational guidelines, opening bank accounts, networking, and government liaison. They have gradually evolved and strengthened their capacity over the years.

To date, 105 such community-based organisations are operating with a total of 2,751 members. Of these, 1,998 are men and 753 women. They are contributing towards making a positive change within their communities in various ways such as organising cultural events and sports, and lobbying with the local government institutions, schools, and others. They are also building relationships with Bengali communities and networking with other organisations such as locally elected bodies, unions, and the local market community, with the aim of countering prejudice and discrimination.

Adibashi land campaign

Shortage of land is a key cause of rural poverty in Bangladesh. The government operates a system of *khash* land, which is supposed to be allocated to poor people who don't own any land. All too often, however, this land is actually taken by wealthy and influential local landowners in the name of the landless, with the assistance of corrupt land officials, members of the local administration, and political leaders.

The poor landless *adibashi* people of Godagari learned of a piece of *khash* land, illegally occupied by a wealthy Bengali, in the nearest village. They contacted Oxfam GB partner Adibashi Unnayan Songstha, who investigated and found that it was indeed *khash* land. They then supported the landless people in submitting an application to the local land office. They also managed to contact the local trade union, local administration, local community leaders, and other authorities.

As a result, 25 landless families from ten different villages settled on the *khash* land. At first, the illegal occupier did not want to give up his illegal possession of the land and tried to intimidate the families. He tried to knock down the newly built *adibashi* houses and to keep possession of the land by offering bribes to the different offices. But as a result of the community's efforts, he had to give up the land. At present, the families are living on the land and trying to complete the settlement process following proper legal procedures. 'We are very happy to be getting a piece of land to take shelter from our difficulties', says Parulbala, one of the people who has settled on the Godagari land.[9]

Reclaiming land can be a very risky process for all vulnerable groups. However, through working as community-based organisations, the *adbiashi* people have information, strength in numbers, and the support of partner organisations to ensure they claim their rights.

Preventing advance labour and crop sale

Adibashi labourers are often paid at a lower rate than Bengali labourers, and women are paid at a lower rate again. It is very common for *adibashi* people to sell their labour and crops in advance to make ends meet during lean periods. Advance labour is sold at lower rates, so when the harvest comes labourers have already been paid, but not at the going rate. As a result, each family loses between 30 and 50 per cent of their total wages annually. To prevent this happening, Oxfam provides soft loans to the community, motivating them to take their own initiatives to reduce their vulnerability.

So *adibashi* peoples were able to reduce their exploitation during lean periods. Now they no longer have to sell their labour and crops in advance and are more able to depend on their own resources.

> **Banking rice for a rainy day**
>
> More than 250 *adibashi* families live in the village of Dewanpur. They are day labourers working in agriculture, where seasonal unemployment is a severe problem. At least twice a year, they become unemployed. As a result, they are compelled to take loans from non-formal sources and sell advance labour and crops at very cheap prices in order to survive. The community-based organisation Barendrabhumi Social Development Organisation (BSDO) aims to prevent this by trying to motivate the villagers to join together and save rice.
>
> Each family saves a handful (250g) of rice a week. One person is appointed to do the accounts for each family with help from BSDO staff and Dewanpur Adibashi Sangstha, a community organisation. To date, 52 maunds (a maund is around 37kg) of rice have been collected by 94 families.
>
> When they have no work, the families can use the rice they have saved and repay it once they have employment. The activity thus functions as a rice bank. So far, the families involved have not had to sell their labour in advance.
>
> 'Annual Report', Indigenous People's Capacity Building Programme, Oxfam GB, July 2006 to June 2007

Policy achievements and recommendations

Through these programme activities, the *adibashi* people who live in the northern plains of Bangladesh have also gained access to policy makers. In some regions, they are included as active participants in development efforts undertaken by other development agencies and by government. *Adibashi* issues have been recognised in the Poverty Reduction Strategy Paper (PRSP) documents. At local level, 11 special standing committees have been formed to address and involve *adibashis* in decision-making bodies. A number of *adibashi* women and men have been included in the primary-school management committee, *khash* land-distribution committees, the security committee, and anti-corruption committees.

This programme shows how the right to be heard has begun to change the lives of the *adibashis*, giving them a voice in what happens to them. For this to continue, the following recommendations should be heeded:

1   Campaigning, awareness-raising, and information-sharing with mainstream communities, authorities, and decision-makers should be increased. It is essential that an enabling environment for the social and economic development of *adibashis* is created and mistrust and social barriers are reduced.

2   Advocacy initiatives to ensure minority groups' rights and needs should be integrated into government, donor, United Nations, NGO, and international NGO development plans and humanitarian initiatives. It is vital that issues are picked up and

addressed through existing networks, as stand-alone campaigns usually have a limited impact.

3   Further investment, leadership, and capacity-building of *adibashi*s is required to sustain the relationship that has been built between the *adibashi* community and local government.

4   High-quality research and information should be maintained as this is crucial for promoting understanding of *adibashi* people and can be used very effectively with allies, the media, and key influencers.

5   Women's leadership in decision-making processes should continue to be strengthened.

6   As there is no model for development for the *adibashi* communities in Bangladesh, the success of this rights-based approach needs to be continally adapted, monitored, evaluated, and shared with others.

7   The learning from this programme also needs to be applied to the other vulnerable groups in Bangladesh, such as particular occupational groups and religious minorities, who constitute almost 19.8 per cent of the population (13 per cent minorities, 1.2 per cent *adibashis*, and 5 per cent occupational).[10]

8   National and international NGOs can play an advocacy role in influencing the United Nations and other donor agencies to comply with their policies and commitments to support development projects with indigenous peoples in Bangladesh.

Notes

[1] Minority Rights International, World Directory of Minorities and Indigenous Peoples, www.minorityrights.org/?lid=5636 (last accessed September 2008).

[2] UNDP, 'Bangladesh: The Human Development Index – Going Beyond Income', http://hdrstats.undp.org/countries/country_fact_sheets/cty_fs_BGD.html (last accessed September 2008).

[3] Oxfam GB, 'Oxfam's Work in Bangladesh in Depth: Work with Indigenous People', www.oxfam.org.uk/resources/countries/bangladesh_indigenous.htm (last accessed September 2008) and Bangladesh Country Brochure (internal).

[4] The ILO Indigenous and Tribal Populations Convention (1957), the UN Convention on the Rights of the Child (1990), the UN International Covenant on Economic, Social, and Cultural Rights (1999), and the UN International Covenant on Civil and Political Rights (2000).

[5] VSO, 'Where we do it – Bangladesh', www.vso.org.uk/about/cprofiles/bangladesh.asp (last accessed September 2008).

[6] From various newspapers: *The Daily Star* (May 2008), *New Age* (May 2008), *Adibashi Jonopother Pothe-prantore* (edited by Joyonto Acharjee (2005), *New Age* (November 2003), and *Weekly 2000* (2004).

[7] Danish International Development Agency, Ministry of Foreign Affairs, Denmark.

[8] Oxfam (2006) internal brochure 'Being that Change in Bangladesh'.

[9] Oxfam GB, Indigenous People's Capacity Building Programme Brochure 2006 (internal).

[10] Bangladesh Bureau of Statistics, www.bbs.gov.bd (last accessed September 2008); Bangladesh Adibashi Forum Report; and MJF Bangladesh, www.mjffoundation.org (last accessed September 2008).

Cover photograph: Ben Beaumont/Oxfam GB 2008

Oxfam GB

Oxfam GB is a development, relief, and campaigning organisation that works with others to find lasting solutions to poverty and suffering around the world. Oxfam GB is a member of Oxfam International.

Oxfam House
John Smith Drive
Cowley
Oxford
OX4 2JY
Tel: +44.(0)1865.473727
E-mail: enquiries@oxfam.org.uk
www.oxfam.org.uk

6. A New Way of Working

Community participation in local budgeting in Georgia

Budget-monitoring group draw a map to highlight problems in a nearby village

The collapse of the Soviet Union led to difficult times for the independent state of Georgia, as it made the transition from a centralised to a market economy, and from a communist to a democratic system. People had no experience of making decisions, even at local level, or of participating actively in local government. Since 2002, Oxfam GB has worked with the Association of Disabled Women and Mothers of Disabled Children with initial support from the Association of Young Economists of Georgia, to implement budget-monitoring projects in Zugdidi District, one of the poorest regions of the country. This paper shows how this process helped communities build the confidence to work directly with local government officials to build a new kind of civil society.

Introduction

Georgia is a nation of some 4.6 million people and it lies between the Black and the Caspian Seas. Like many other states or former Soviet republics, it became independent after the collapse of the Soviet Union in 1991. This meant moving from a centralised to a market economy, and from a communist to a democratic system. The result was a political and economic crisis, during which many people became impoverished. In addition, civil war and the internal conflicts of the early 1990s created more than 300,000 internally displaced people (IDPs) from two breakaway regions: Abkhazia and South Ossetia.[1]

By the mid 1990s the government had managed to restore stability and peace. The economy started to pick up and there appeared to be hope for a brighter future. However, the government led by the former Soviet minister of foreign affairs – President Eduard Shevardnadze – proved to be too corrupt, ineffective, and inept at setting the country on course towards building a just, equal, and prosperous society. At the dawn of the twenty-first century, Georgia, often dubbed a 'failing state', found itself on the verge of the utter disintegration of its political and socio-economic fabric.

In November 2003, tens of thousands of demonstrators took to the streets in a peaceful protest known as the Rose Revolution. The beleaguered regime of President Shevardnadze was toppled. Since then, a number of positive changes have taken place in the country. One of the most obvious is an improved and rehabilitated infrastructure. However, other problems remain, for example inflation is high. Corruption was a major problem in the Soviet system. The government announced a crackdown in 2005 and managed to significantly reduce the level of administrative or so-called 'petty' corruption. However, it remains a problem. In 2007, Georgia was ranked 79th in Transparency International's Corruption Perception Index, with a score of 2.8 out of 10 (where 10 means no evidence of corruption). Social inequality is increasing – there is practically no middle class in Georgian society, and large numbers of people are unemployed.[2] The needs of poor people continue to be ignored. Growing discontent led to mass protests and upheaval in November 2007. This resulted in the government announcing an emergency situation and a call for new presidential elections, which were held in January 2008, followed by the parliamentary elections in May 2008.

In August 2008, armed conflict between Russia and Georgia broke out over Georgia's breakaway regions of Abkhazia and South Ossetia. Heavy fighting resulted in large numbers of ethnic Georgians being forced to leave their homes, thus turning them into IDPs within Georgia. Russian forces carved out the so-called security zones within Georgia, having occupied strategic places inside the country. The conflict left many civilian casualties. As of October 2008, Russian troops withdrew from the undisputed Georgian territories, but they still remain inside Abkhazia and South Ossetia, which Russia now recognises as independent states.[3]

This recent conflict and unrest has not helped with Georgia's efforts to reduce poverty, as the country's resources have been focused on the conflict and those who have lost their homes and health as a result. On re-election in May, the president and his government proclaimed poverty reduction as its priority. However, this may prove much harder than expected in the light of recent events. The re-elected government brought some new, educated, and energetic people to lead the reform process aimed at poverty alleviation. Many of these people often lack experience and the knowledge of poor people's needs and priorities. But this aspiration of lifting the country out of poverty is where the interests of the political leadership and the interests of development-oriented international and local agencies converge. Interference and public criticism by international agencies and donors provokes strong reactions from politicians, but the government is keen to impress the international community with its commitment to neo-liberalism and reform. So the international community can significantly influence decision-making at all levels. This is the area in which Oxfam and its partner civil-society organisations strive to bring about change.

Changing attitudes: local self-governance

In 1998, the government attempted a decentralisation process through local government reforms, which gave more power to elected representatives of the local self-governance body, the *Sakrebulo*. The role of these bodies is to listen to what people have to say at local level, monitor what is happening, and make proposals for change. These proposals are then taken to the *Gamgeoba*, the executive branch of local self-governance, and if necessary to central government. Resources can then flow back to the villages and municipalities.

However, political turmoil meant that it was not possible to carry out proper reforms or real decentralisation. As a result, self-governance remained weak and the local population disengaged. This meant that the interests of the local population, especially the most vulnerable, were still not reflected in local decision-making processes.

This was the context when Oxfam GB started mobilising local communities in 2002 to engage with local representatives. Changing attitudes to participation was not going to be an easy task, so Oxfam ran a pilot project to empower local communities. Through participation in budget monitoring and budget formation, people would become engaged in the decisions taken in their communities and begin to feel that their active participation could change things.

Between 2002 and 2004, Oxfam GB worked with the Association of Disabled Women and Mothers of Disabled Children (DEA) and the Association of Young Economists of Georgia (AYEG)[4] to implement budget-monitoring projects in Zugdidi, one of the poorest areas in Georgia with many displaced people from neighbouring Abkhazia. While DEA carried out the local work, AYEG worked more at national level.

DEA was originally set up by Madonna Kharebava (a disabled woman) with the aim of ensuring that disabled people had a voice in local decisions. The organisation started by focusing on social spending and how the budget was being used for disabled people, and gradually expanded to include other areas of government spending. As capacity grew, DEA extended its scope to include all local people in the creation of local community groups to monitor budgets, which resulted in the birth of the Local Budget Monitoring project.

Raising awarness and building trust: the Local Budget Monitoring project

Between 2006 to 2008, DEA ran the Local Budget Monitoring project, which aimed to institutionalise the participation of civil society in local government in Zugdidi, a municipality in western Georgia comprising more than 30 villages. The objectives were to:

- Improve the skills and raise the awareness of local government representatives

- Introduce participatory attitudes and principles into budgetary processes

- Conduct budget monitoring of the budget of Zugdidi municipality in 2007 and part of 2008

- Raise public awareness about budgetary processes and budget monitoring.

DEA worked closely with both the *Sakrebulo* and the *Gamgeoba*. With the elected representatives, DEA focused mainly on capacity-building, training, and making the representatives more aware of the laws and functions they can work with. With the *Gamgeoba*, the focus was more on lobbying for the correct use of the budget and trying to ensure that they prioritise local demands.

During the two years of the project, DEA mobilised the local population in all 30 villages, and established interest groups in each, made up of ten to 15 socially active villagers. Interest groups were groups of local people who wanted to get together to either influence, or participate in, the developments of their community. However, they did not have the skills or practical experience to participate in local budget monitoring, and so groups of committed individuals formed community committees.

DEA assisted these committees to develop statutes, co-ordinated twice-monthly meetings, and, together with AYEG,[5] conducted local budget-monitoring training. AYEG's role at the start of the project was very important in providing capacity-building training and training in grassroots advocacy and lobbying, as well as assisting DEA in analysing the budget data they managed to collect. The goal was to develop the skills and abilities of committee members on budgetary process issues, as well as helping them to understand both organs of local self-governance, and to undertake advocacy and lobbying. The committees prepared their suggestions, recommendations, and initiatives and submitted these to the *Gamgeoba*.

The idea was to build a new kind of civil society, where each member would feel responsible for the community's budget and be capable of participating in its formation, based on the needs of a particular community.

Believing in budgets

An 18-year-old woman, Lana Korshia, who is a member of the local budget-monitoring group in the village of Tsaishi, said: 'Gradually, I became so interested in budgetary processes that I could not refrain from discussing our local budget with my peers. This obsession looked weird for someone of my age, in the beginning my counterparts and friends were not interested, but now I have interested them so much that they themselves ask questions about local and national budgets. I am very proud'.

Lia, a member of the committee from the village of Akhalsopeli, Zugdidi District, says: 'I would be lying to you if I said that the community liked or trusted budget monitoring from the beginning, many of them even questioned what one villager can do in such a chaos where a *Sakrebulo* member is not able to address the problem. Information obtained during the past years made us believe that we can stand up for our interests and take steps in order to tackle specific problems'.

As a result of the mobilisation and inclusion of villagers in the budget-monitoring work, as well as the capacity-building they received, people grew more confident and felt more empowered. The community groups were very successful in working directly with local government. Since 2005, 85 per cent of recommendations from the committees have been taken on board. The relationships between local self-governance representatives and communities improved, and there was increased transparency in the budgetary process. People have started to have more trust in their local government. Members of the Local Budget Monitoring project have even been offered some office space in the Zugdidi local self-governance building, to set up a resource centre that will provide the population with information on the new tax code, budgetary processes, and other enquiries. This is clear evidence that the local government is satisfied with the project.

The new law on local self-governance

On 16 December 2005, Georgia's Parliament adopted a new law on local self-governance, which defines the legal, economic, and financial basis of local self-governance, as well as state guarantees, rules for the establishment of local self-governance, and their responsibilities and relations with state authorities. On the basis of the new law, on 5 October 2006, local elections were held for people to choose their self-governance representatives.

The reform changed the structure of the local self-governance system, removing the lowest administrative division and effectively abolishing local self-governance in communities, annulling community budgets.

The new arrangement gives each Georgian city and its surrounding villages municipality status, with local self-governance. The only exceptions are Tbilisi, the capital, Batumi, the capital of the Autonomous Republic of Adjara, and other major cities like Poti, Rustavi, and Kutaisi.

This change had its positive side, which was to make the system more flexible to manage, but at the same time it has negative ones – it is possible that local authorities will become further isolated and detached from the local population. However, the new law obliges municipalities to ensure the active participation of society, seek ways of co-operation with them, and ensure transparency, accountability, socio-economic development, civil participation, and improvement of living standards, especially for vulnerable people.

However, adopting new laws, making changes to the existing imperfect legislation, and giving people the opportunity to participate in elections, is not enough to strengthen local self-governance. The whole style of self-governance needs to change, and modern management methods introduced. This means increasing the effectiveness of local government, which can be achieved partly through the promotion of an active civil society.

After the reforms

In Zugdidi, before the new law, each of the 30 villages had its own local self-governance unit. After 2006, the city of Zugdidi and its villages became a single municipality. There was now only one budget for the whole municipality rather than one for each village.

The Local Budget Monitoring project therefore decided to transform all local community groups and community committees into one public municipality committee that would monitor the Zugdidi municipality budget. People of different ages, professions, districts, and social strata (among them vulnerable people and IDPs) were involved.

In consultation with the community, the public municipality committee developed its own statute. It keeps the community informed and has divided itself into six thematic monitoring groups. These are:

1 The rule of law

2 Education, culture, and sports

3 The social sphere

4 Property and privatisation

5 Infrastructure

6 Gender budget monitoring.

These groups correspond to the committees in the Zugdidi municipality, the *Gamgeoba*, and the *Sakrebulo*, except for the gender budget monitoring committee, which is unique to the project. There are up to 13 members in each group, involving approximately 75 people. Each thematic group has its own strategy, on the basis of which action plans are developed. Thematic group members submit priorities to the *Gamgeoba* and the *Sakrebulo*.

After the local elections in 2006, DEA conducted a survey targeting representatives of Zugdidi municipality *Sakrebulo* and society as a whole. The results showed that many newly elected members lacked the experience and skills needed to undertake their work and to co-operate with civil society. They were also hampered by the fact that legislation is spread through many legal documents and so is difficult to access and interpret. This leaves local people at a disadvantage.

The survey showed that there were three specific needs that were within the capacity and reach of DEA's work: raising awareness; increasing the competence of local representatives; and participatory budgeting as a key to increasing accountability.

Raising awareness

DEA and the public committee found several ways of disseminating information to civil society. These included:

- Quarterly bulletins highlighting the results of the Zugdidi municipality budget monitoring, as well as information in easily understandable language and explanations about self-governance issues and *Sakrebulo* decisions. The bulletin includes space for legal advice. It is disseminated among local organisations working on similar issues, and to all nine municipalities in the

Samegrelo region and the main library of the Samegrelo-Zemo Svaneti region.

- Radio programmes broadcast twice a month by local radio station *Atinati*, which covers the whole of western Georgia including Sokhumi, the capital of the breakaway republic of Abkhazia.

- DEA uses its own publication – the newspaper *Natlis Sveti*, to disseminate the results of the public discussions and budget monitoring.

Ordinary villagers find it very useful to be able to access such information.

Seeing for myself

Geronti, a 64-year-old man from the village of Akhalabastumani, says: 'Earlier I was not interested in these issues, I did not even know what the amount of the district budget was. Now, I take an interest in budgetary processes; moreover, I know where to find the information. We receive quarterly bulletins on a regular basis, which clearly reflect the issues of self-governance and budgetary processes, legislative changes. Along with other participants I took part in the radio programme "Community and Budget" and saw for myself the feedback from our broadcasts, as well as live discussions about acute problems in our communities'.

Increasing the competence of local representatives

Members of the public committee are trained in self-governance issues, including budgeting and issues relating to property and the privatisation of agricultural lands, which is a key problem in 2008. Land-privatisation issues are very important for the population of Zugdidi, because agricultural land is the only surviving resource against a backdrop of high unemployment. Lack of agricultural land is one of the reasons for migration of young people from the region, which means that there are fewer people to work in the villages and on the land. Land privatisation, which was meant to be a public and transparent process, was not carried out in Zugdidi in a transparent manner. Therefore, the population were eager to get more information and capacity-building resources in order to feel more confident and able to fully engage in the process.

Valeri (a middle-aged man) from the village of Urta, a member of the public monitoring committee on land-privatisation issues, says: 'The privatisation process taking place in Zugdidi municipality is very faulty indeed. All of us know that this is not going to be a painless process, therefore it is doubly important to inform the villagers on these issues. Information is not accessible to them, helpless peasants and farmers are not aware of the rights they have to the agricultural land. In such circumstances public monitoring is the only effective way to protect the interests of the population and their lawful rights. We, as members of the public monitoring group, should have all the answers not only to the legal aspects of the privatisation, but also should be informed of the steps taken by the local self-governance. Although obtaining relevant and precise information is getting more and more difficult, the population of Zugdidi villages of Anaklia, Chkhoria, and Chitatskari are expressing their dissatisfaction regarding Italian investors who want to buy all the agricultural land belonging to these villages. Local authorities, in their turn, point fingers at the Ministry of Economic Development. We believe that the solution is very simple: no one should hide information that is supposed to be public'.

Tengiz, a member of the public committee and a resident of the village of Didinedzi, says: 'If not for the information received about the issues of land privatisation within the project, our community residents would not be able to get involved in the land privatisation process, and accordingly we would have remained beyond the whole process of privatisation'.

Training was also conducted for representatives of the *Sakrebulo* and *Gamgeoba*. Topics were selected, taking members' opinions into consideration. As a result of the training, members' skills and knowledge about budgetary and monitoring processes, self-governance, preparing project proposals, advocacy and lobbying, privatisation of state-owned agricultural lands, as well as issues concerning state purchases, were improved.

Participatory budgeting as a key to increasing accountability

One of the reasons why the needs of poor people are not part of budget formation and programme planning is the fact that they themselves are not aware of their rights. The participation of the local population in budgeting engages civil society, especially vulnerable people, in local government. This then has a positive effect on poverty reduction, and stimulates civil society to participate in addressing the country's problems.

DEA involved women in the budget-monitoring work at community level and ensured that the impact of public expenditures on women and men was analysed. Georgian women traditionally play an active part in society; one of the successes of the project has been that more women are becoming engaged in these local budget issues; out of 56 individuals on the eight public committees, 34 are women.

An evaluation showed that the government was positive about the project, and that the attitudes of local authorities towards public participation are changing. A memorandum of mutual understanding was developed between the public committee and Zugdidi municipality representatives, stipulating that the *Gamgeoba*, the *Sakrebulo*, and DEA would co-operate to further develop the self-governance system and ensure public participation.

As Petre Antia, a member of Zugdidi municipality *Sakrebulo*, said: 'Our first contact with civil committees assured us that we dealt with people who are well aware of the situation and have definitely thought about the problems faced by communities. We welcome the goodwill of DEA to facilitate the active participation of society'.

This sort of attitude is quite unusual for the representatives of the local authorities in other parts of Georgia, where they are mostly isolated, have little contact with the grassroots, and take decisions unilaterally, without including the local population in decision-making processes.

Bridging the gap: community social projects

Another area of work that has great potential for the project is involving the communities in micro social projects such as fixing village roads; restoring green areas or forests; or removing waste and cleaning up villages. This encourages community involvement and builds skills such as the ability to prioritise and identify resources. It also builds involvement with, and understanding of, the local self-governance structures.

The members of the public committee represent their village and bring these problems to the committee. Together they developed a 'problems map' for all 30 villages of Zugdidi region and then prioritised how to solve these problems with the help of resources requested from local authorities and the village community itself. The public committee and the 'problems map' serve as a link between the grassroots and the local authorities, thus representing the voices of the most vulnerable people in that society. At the same time, the villagers realise that it is not effective to sit and wait until their problems are solved from the top. Instead, they come forward with specific solutions, lobby for their projects, and show their own solutions to the problems, which can then be solved.

Building roads and bridges

In the village of Narazeni, a 3km stretch of the road over the river Umpa was badly damaged. It was difficult to use even on foot, and practically impossible in a vehicle. Maka Kalichava and Nato Todua, two women members of the public committee who lived in the village, noted that because of this the village was isolated from the rest of the world, since the road over the bridge is the only means to get to the city of Zugdidi and other villages. This was causing especially severe problems for 28 schoolchildren living in the area because it meant they could not use public transport but had to walk several kilometres to get to school. The community expressed their willingness to help. The committee members proposed that local authorities should provide resources for construction vehicles and fuel, as well as permission to extract crushed rock from the bottom of another river to fill and patch the gaps. This was agreed and as a result the road-construction work began.

The public committee, together with DEA, prepared a number of these community projects, successfully bringing the needs of the community, and what they are prepared to contribute, to the attention of the municipality. Communities are now starting to believe they can change things in this way if they are willing to work towards a common goal.

Nazi Aronia, an ex-Member of Parliament from the ruling party, was invited to the public committee discussion. She was impressed with the power and perseverance of the group, saying: 'We were pleasantly surprised about the level of the public committee's awareness, their views of the problems, the suggestions and recommendations they provided, and their sense of reality, all of which were revealed during the meeting. Consultation and suggestions of such people will positively influence our common activities'.

Conclusion and lessons learned

The Local Budget Monitoring project is very new for people in Georgia, where it has always been difficult to introduce principles of transparency and accountability in communities. The project had many successes, both large and small. Here we concentrate on some of the major ones.

Probably the most important success had to do with attitudinal change; ensuring that people moved from the passive expectation that everything would be done for them from the top, to believing that they could have an active say in the decisions that affected their lives. The project has resulted in obvious changes in people's attitudes and approaches, and they have a greater sense of responsibility towards the needs of their communities.

Information and training were key to the success of the project. Communities were given a chance to get acquainted with local and district budgets before the changes to the self-governance system, and later, after the reform in 2006, with the Zugdidi District municipal budget. They were given regular information on budgets by experts. The local population now knows what the duties and responsibilities of the community and local government are in budgetary processes.

As a result of all these factors, for the first time, communities in Zugdidi were able to participate in the monitoring of municipal budgets. Negative expectations and suspicion were replaced with co-operation between communities and public municipality committees, building a whole new way of working. The process of changing civil society can be slow and difficult, but this project demonstrated that it can be done.

In terms of future plans, the mobilised public monitoring committee will continue budget-monitoring activities. The goal is to engage more people, especially young people, in local budgetary issues, and to continue capacity-building for local authorities in order to improve their accountability and transparency. In 2008, a youth centre project was established within the Municipalities Building in the centre of Zugdidi. However, during the war, Russian soldiers occupied this building and therefore for security reasons it was decided to move the youth centre to the premises of DEA. An empowered local population (in particular, young people) will play a crucial role in rebuilding broken Georgia.

Notes

[1] Note that after the August 2008 war, IDP numbers increased by around 190,000. See Internal Displacement Monitoring Centre, 'Georgia', www.internal-displacement.org/idmc/website/countries.nsf/(httpEnvelopes)/ 234CB919545031A9C12571D2004E4F73?OpenDocument#sources (last accessed September 2008). Some 300,000 people fled conflicts in or were expelled from Abkhazia and South Ossetia in the early 1990s. Some 45,000 of them returned to Gali, Abkhazia a few years ago. Since then, the number of IDPs has not decreased, as children of IDPs are also counted as IDPs. In 2004–2005 the Ministry of Refugees and Accommodation (MRA), with the support of UNHCR and of the Swiss government, undertook a verification exercise to update the number of IDPs. Some 221,000 people were verified, but this number has not been endorsed by Georgian authorities, who used the estimate of 247,000 as of early 2007. Also, the Georgian government has started registering some of the hundreds of Georgian citizens recently deported from Russia as IDPs. See also Government of Georgia (2007) 'Decree # 47', www.internal-displacement.org/8025708F004CE90B/(httpDocuments)/0860F04B3162B38 CC12572950056DBED/$file/State+Strategy+for+IDP+-+ENG.pdf (last accessed September 2008).

[2] According to official statistics the number of unemployed people in Georgia is 274,500 (13.6 per cent). However, unofficial statistics vary: experts place it as high as 25 per cent. See www.parliament.ge/index.php?lang_id= ENG&sec_id=327 and Ministry of Economic Development of Georgia (2007) 'Statistical Yearbook of Georgia 2007', page 328: www.statistics.ge/ _files/yearbook/Yearbook_2007.pdf (both last accessed September 2008).

[3] BBC News Website – http://news.bbc.co.uk/1/hi/world/europe/7658385.stm (last accessed October 2008)

[4] Note that AYEG were only involved in the budget-monitoring project in the early stages.

[5] AYEG is currently conducting participatory monitoring of state social policy. It works in collaboration with state agencies to help reveal the challenges of the state social-assistance programme and the Social Subsidies Agency allocation, and to try to ensure the process is participatory and transparent. Oxfam has been involved in this project since 2005. The project comprises monitoring of programme implementation; conducting qualitative, quantitative, and panel surveys throughout the project year; and developing recommendations which are then communicated to the Agency.

Cover photograph: Louise Lewis/Oxfam 2007

© Oxfam GB, November 2008

This paper was written by Thea Jamaspishvili. Thank you to Nikki van der Gaag who edited the paper and to Emily Laurie who provided research assistance. It is part of a series of papers written to inform public debate on development and humanitarian policy issues. The text may be freely used for the purposes of campaigning, education, and research, provided that the source is acknowledged in full.

For further information please email: publish@oxfam.org.uk

Online ISBN 978-1-84814-061-5. This paper is part of a set **Speaking Out: How the voices of poor people are shaping the future** available for purchase from Oxfam Publishing or its agents, print ISBN 978-0-85598-638-4 for the set of 12 papers. For more information visit http://publications.oxfam.org.uk/oxfam/display.asp?ISBN=9780855986384

This paper is also available in French and Spanish.

Oxfam GB

Oxfam GB is a development, relief, and campaigning organisation that works with others to find lasting solutions to poverty and suffering around the world. Oxfam GB is a member of Oxfam International.

Oxfam House
John Smith Drive
Cowley
Oxford
OX4 2JY

Tel: +44.(0)1865.473727
E-mail: enquiries@oxfam.org.uk
www.oxfam.org.uk

7. Indigenous Women against Impunity

Challenging discrimination in Guatemala's legal system

Women register at the Rights of Indigenous People's Workshop in Patzité

Guatemala signed a peace accord in 1997, after 36 years of conflict. But the legacy of violence continues to haunt its population, especially indigenous people and women, who face ethnic and gender-based discrimination. A culture of impunity dominates the government's legal system. Only 3 per cent of violent deaths are ever investigated. Violence, especially violence against women, is escalating. Indigenous people in Guatemala have their own traditional justice system, which operates alongside that of the state, although not on an equal legal footing. This paper looks at the relative successes of traditional conflict-resolution mechanisms, and examines how indigenous women are using Indigenous People's Defence Organisations to seek justice.

Introduction

Guatemala suffered from almost four decades of armed conflict, which ended in a peace accord in 1997. During this time, more than 200,000 people were killed or disappeared. Most were civilians, and 83 per cent were indigenous people.[1] The legacy of this violence continues today. Social relationships are characterised by aggression and violence, and the government is directly or indirectly responsible for many different kinds of abuses. The country ranks 118th out of 177 in the latest United Nations Human Development Report. More than half the population lives in poverty, and 15.6 per cent in extreme poverty.[2]

United Nations Human Rights High Commissioner, Louise Arbour, described Guatemala as 'one of the most violent countries in the region'.[3] Since 2001, violent homicides have increased by 120 per cent.[4] In 2007, there were more than 5,000 violent deaths. Firearms were used in 80 per cent of cases. There are two million individual firearms in a country of 13 million people, reflecting the general climate of insecurity.

Indigenous people, who make up 42 per cent of the population, are considered second-class citizens and face some of the most serious discrimination and abuse. Seventy-five per cent live in poverty, compared with 38 per cent of the non-indigenous populations.[5] Forty-eight per cent are illiterate, compared with 30 per cent of the non-indigenous population. For indigenous women, illiteracy is higher, at 65 per cent.[6]

Women in particular face violence, discrimination, and oppression: Guatemala is 127th out of 156 in the most recent United Nations Gender Development Index. Although the country has a legal framework of 14 documents specifying the protection of women's rights, belief in the superiority of men over women, coupled with traditional social practices, lead to many injustices and human-rights violations against women, especially indigenous women.[7]

Guatemala has the highest rate of women homicides in the Americas and the fifth in the world.[8] Between 2000 and 2007, almost 4,000 women were murdered. In most of these murders, the criminal's rage is unmistakable, as victims are often raped and sexually assaulted. Bodies with these characteristics appear daily in ravines, on the street, in desolate places, or in the victim's own home.[9] Every two days, a young girl dies a violent death, 80 per cent of them sexually assaulted. Two per cent are under the age of five.[10]

A culture of impunity

Despite the high levels of crime and homicide, few criminals are brought to justice. Ninety-seven per cent of homicides are not investigated; a figure that glaringly demonstrates the degree of impunity that exists in the country. In addition to protecting criminals, impunity encourages crime as a way to solve problems and conflicts through violent means, individually or collectively through lynching.

'Where impunity is the rule for past violations, it should come as no surprise that it also prevails for current crimes', says Louise Arbour.[11] Angie Hougas of Amnesty International explains: 'Impunity sends the message that ill treatment and torture of people will be tolerated. It denies victims justice and it erodes public confidence in its judicial system. It is a breakdown in the judicial system; it affects our outlook and undermines our trust in the whole criminal justice process. The effect of this is, it impedes the path to peace and respect for human rights, human worth and human dignity'.[12]

The inability and inefficiency of the Guatemalan system in delivering justice has resulted in high levels of frustration among the general population, which leads to apathy. The United Nations in Guatemala estimates that 75 per cent of crimes are not reported, mostly because victims consider that 'it is not worth it', or because they are afraid of retaliation.[13]

These are the consequences of a centralised, bureaucratic model which is slow, expensive, and has insufficient coverage; a system which abandons the victims and repeatedly violates due process.[14] The police force and other authorities of justice are frequently accused of corruption, extra-judicial executions, torture, abuse of authority, negligence, and discrimination. No administrative or judicial action is taken against them so far, which in turn protects them and encourages impunity on behalf of the very institutions that should be fighting it.

'The institutional collapse in the distribution of justice is not due to a lack of material and qualified human resources. The magnitude of impunity in Guatemala is the result of the State's inability to purge clandestine groups from within these institutions which have been controlling them since the armed conflict and have the power to neutralise them', says Carlos Castresana, Director of the International Commission Against Impunity in Guatemala.[15]

The official justice system in Guatemala is rampant with racism and sexism, and does not adequately address any cases involving indigenous people and women, particularly indigenous women. Indigenous people have even less chance of finding justice than the rest of the population: the system obstructs access to justice and violates human rights through its instruments and legal processes.

For example, research found that many indigenous people spend up to ten months in prison without being processed and/or sentenced, even when they are innocent.[16] Even though 23 indigenous languages are spoken, a multilingual justice system does not exist, interpretation services are insufficient, and there is a lack of bilingual operators.[17] Spanish being the official language is an obstacle, as 'those who are illiterate or who do not speak or understand Spanish' cannot officially act as witnesses.[18] This excludes illiterate people (30 per cent of the population) and the monolingual indigenous population (more than one million people).

According to Alexei Avtonomov, Rapporteur for Guatemala, United Nations Committee on the Elimination of Racial Discrimination: 'Disdain and rejection towards the indigenous population is evident among several sectors. It is necessary to develop instruments that allow access to justice, so as to overcome the high levels of discrimination and facilitate the implementation of basic rights for Guatemala's ethnic groups'.[19]

It was in recognition of the seriousness of this situation that in late December 2006, the Guatemalan government and the United Nations signed an agreement to establish the International Commission against Impunity in Guatemala (Comisión Internacional Contra la Impunidad en Guatemala – CICIG), to assist local authorities in investigating and dismantling the clandestine groups. The International Commission, the first of its kind in the world, began to operate in January 2008. It is hoped that this will begin to address some of the major issues within the official justice system. In the meantime, indigenous people are working on supporting those whose rights have been violated, not only through the official justice system, but also through a traditional indigenous justice system, which operates alongside the state system.

This paper examines how indigenous people are using their own traditional justice systems to address rights abuses and the culture of impunity, and at the same time ensuring that cases are dealt with through the state justice system and the courts.

The right to judicial pluralism

The 1996 Agreement between the Guatemalan government and the guerillas states that: 'For indigenous people, traditional norms have been, and continue to be, a basic element for the social regulation of life in their communities and therefore, for the maintenance of their unity.'[20] Indigenous law has survived five centuries of colonisation.[21] Indigenous justice is not based on punishment, but is seen as a guide and an educational process that helps communities to: 'avoid and amend inappropriate conduct or wrong actions'.[22] It takes into account the interests and relationships of those in dispute, searching for compensation, balance, and harmony.

Guatemala has committed to respecting the rights of indigenous people and their judicial system, signing international agreements such as Convention 169 of the International Labour Organisation, the International Convention to Eliminate all Forms of Discrimination and Racism, and the Declaration for Universal Indigenous People's Rights. Pursuing these rights as an alternative to a judicial and culturally ethnocentric system represents a real challenge.[23] The legal structure, process, and restrictions of the official justice system go against the essence and implementation of traditional indigenous justice which is oral and educational.

Indigenous traditional justice has survived alongside official state law and is a daily reality in Guatemala. During colonial times, the segregation system allowed the indigenous population to administer their own justice, but they had to submit this to the colonial authorities. This practice was then totally prohibited during Independence (1821) until the most recent Constitution in 1985, which indirectly recognises the obligation of the state to 'respect the customs, traditions and ways of life' of indigenous peoples. Nevertheless, the Constitution establishes that 'any jurisdictional functions can only be attributed to the Supreme Court and other courts, as stated by the law'. The use of indigenous justice was given legitimacy in the 1996 Peace Accords. The Guatemalan state is now formally committed to an official recognition of this system, but legislation still does not recognise this. Even so, 'the implementation of indigenous law has advantages in geographical and linguistic accessibility, and cultural pertinence, privileging reparation and satisfaction of both parts in conflict resolution', according to the Guatemalan office of the United Nations High Commissioner.[24]

Indigenous People's Defence Organisations

Indigenous People's Defence Organisations support indigenous justice systems by directly assisting cases, accompanying complainants to public justice institutions, strengthening indigenous authorities with cultural principles and values, and organising community councils to promote rights in the indigenous regions of Guatemala. They include the Defensoría Indígena Wajxaqib' Noj, Defensoría K'iché, and Defensoría Maya.

Confronting violence against women[27]

Domestic violence is a major problem in Guatemala. In 2007 alone, it was reported by more than 17,000 women.[28] Of the 2,600 women assisted yearly at the government-run Indigenous Women's Defence Office, which co-ordinates and collaborates with the Indigenous People's Defence Organisations, 85 per cent reported family violence, 11 per cent rape, and 4 per cent ethnic discrimination.[29]

But campaigns to have domestic violence treated seriously lack the support of male leaders, and women are often fearful to come forward. 'Women activists say that fear is one of the main problems they face as they try to galvanise people inside Guatemala to pressure the Government to do more', says one newspaper report.[30]

In seeking justice, the petitioner once again becomes a victim, only this time from insensitive authorities who: 'treat rape, murder and cell phone theft the same way', according to one penal system researcher.[31] Amnesty International has documented that the severe and persistent deficiencies of the system, along with discriminatory attitudes on the part of authorities, result in a lack of protection of women at risk, blaming of the victim, and denial of justice.[32]

Indigenous justice systems can claim to have more success: while the government justice system favourably resolves only 3 per cent of all reported cases of domestic violence, the Indigenous People's Defence Organisations have clarified and resolved more than 60 per cent.

On receiving cases of domestic violence, the Defence Organisations first focus on the prevention of more violence and mediating the relationship. Failing this, a separation is advised with shared child-care responsibilities. Other cases come to their attention because they have not been dealt with by the government justice system, such as the case of María Chacaj.

> **María Chacaj**
>
> María Chacaj was a victim of persistent domestic violence who disappeared in June 2006. Her husband reported her 'disappearance', but authorities did not investigate it. Later, he tried to have the matter dismissed saying she had probably 'run off with other men'. The report was filed away and forgotten by the official system. Not convinced, María's family members turned to one of the Indigenous People's Defence Organisations, and with the community's support, in January 2007, her remains were found buried in the patio of their house. Her husband was apprehended the same day by local authorities and handed over to the police.[33] In May 2008, a judge sentenced him to 26 years in prison. In this case, the Indigenous People's Defence Organisation assisted the case in being brought to justice in the official system.

Many other cases have been reported by women to the Defence Organisations for domestic violence, incest, fraud, and to claim their rightful inheritance. One woman said: 'I prefer to come to their offices instead of the court, because they truly help us', and another noted: 'I hope these defence offices never close, because they really help us'.

> **Anastasia Suy**
>
> Anastasia Suy is a widow with five children. She is from the Mayan K'iché ethnic group, part of the 60 per cent monolingual indigenous population,[34] and one of the 75 per cent of indigenous people living in poverty.[35] After the death of her husband four years ago, their land titles were handed over to her mother-in-law by the 'official' court system, despite the fact that she had legal rights to the land. Her community advised her to go to the Indigenous People's Defence Organisation, who assisted in mediation between the two women. She was able to speak in her own language, resolve her litigation through traditional means, and was accompanied to court to legalise the agreement in the 'official' system.
>
> In this way she avoided the institutional bureaucratic paperwork and the high fees charged by lawyers. In November 2007, her mother-in-law agreed to give the land over, although it was put in Anastasia's children's names rather than her own.[36]

The Defence Organisations also complement service provision with activities that favour skills development of indigenous women. They offer leadership training and education about their rights, in order to promote their empowerment, in turn helping them face violence and oppression on all levels. Women interviewed by Oxfam who had been accompanied by the Indigenous People's Defence Organisations highlighted the importance of the attention and accompaniment received, and the results obtained. They valued being believed and understood in their own language.[37] Antonia Buch, President of Defensoría Maya, says she values 'the trust we have gained among the women…many act as replicators of the knowledge acquired through the training'.

The sub co-ordinator of the Defensoría K'iché, Sebastiana Sen, emphasises the advocacy work of organised women, and their participation in the local development councils (LDCs) in order to demand accountability at the municipal level. LDCs are part of a government attempt to decentralise decision-making. They offer, in theory, participation to local leaders at the community and municipal levels.

As women challenge and denounce gender-based oppression and violence, insisting on their rights, they become empowered and their roles become more prominent in society. Women like Antonia, Sebastiana, and Fermina know that results take time, but also that through their work they are seeing advancements in indigenous women's rights in their country and eventually a lessening of the violence.

Oxfam's role

During the 1990s, Oxfam GB supported the work of the Indigenous People's Defence Organisations, in order to protect communities and leaders when their human rights were violated in the context of the armed conflict and military control.

Now, Oxfam GB strengthens the Defence Organisations and indigenous local authorities on a human-rights and gender approach to indigenous women who are victims of violence. Support also includes helping these organisations to focus their strategies so that they can increase the legitimacy of their demands and co-ordinate more effectively with the official authorities.

Recommendations

Oxfam's work to promote the right to be heard includes efforts to improve the ability of marginalised populations to make an impact on decisions that affect their lives. This includes, but is not limited to, ensuring that the state and its justice systems are inclusive and responsive to the needs of diverse populations.

While supporting the efforts of indigenous populations in Guatemala to create more inclusive alternatives to the existing state justice system, major changes in the structure and attitudes of society as a whole are also necessary. The state must guarantee to improve access to justice for indigenous and non-indigenous women, and for Guatemalans in general, in order to stop the systematic proliferation of racist and sexist beliefs and practices. This means improving the institutions designed to promote justice and security, as well as the state's role in educating and promoting rights. New approaches are needed at different levels, with diverse strategies that are culturally appropriate, for example, promoting women's rights linking with the Mayan worldview of equity and respect.

Based on the experience and expertise of the organisations with whom Oxfam works, recommendations are focused on different levels. Implementing these recommendations will mean that the voices and visions of indigenous people are more likely to have an impact on the legal and policy decisions that affect their lives.

International

- Guatemala has an important opportunity to eradicate clandestine and violent groups through the new International Commission Against Impunity in Guatemala. The international community can help in two ways: through financial support to cover operating costs, and political accompaniment to ensure security and efficiency.

- The situation of women and indigenous people in Guatemala should be monitored with assistance from governments and multilateral organisations. This will help to pressurise the Guatemalan government into guaranteeing human rights and promoting an inclusive society where the participation of groups who are discriminated against is improved.

National co-operation and civil society

- The Guatemalan state and its institutions should **restructure the justice system**, putting into place effective policies and practices which combat impunity, racism, and all forms of discrimination; with culturally appropriate processes and services for victims, especially for rural indigenous women.

- The recent **reform of the Penal Code**, which combats violence against women in Guatemala according to international human-rights standards, needs to be applied in practice. The government must accept and carry out the recommendations of the United Nations High Commissioner for Human Rights.

- **Indigenous authorities** should be sensitive towards victims of violence and ensure that they offer conditions for their protection and the right to a life free of violence.

- The right to be heard for indigenous and non-indigenous women should be promoted through **literacy programmes**, which support the use of their native language, and help them to understand and demand their rights within their families, communities, and the state.

- The **organisations of women survivors** of violence should be supported in order to ensure their self-esteem, economic empowerment, and access to basic services, as well as justice. The role of indigenous women within the Defence Organisations should be strengthened as a way of striving toward gender equity in the face of cultural oppression and exclusion.

- **Indigenous justice** should be supported and strengthened through the Indigenous People's Defence Organisations as a legitimate and recognised alternative system. **The level of co-ordination** with official authorities should be raised to ensure effective and culturally appropriate approaches to violence against indigenous women, as well as other conflicts that affect these communities. Official and indigenous authorities must talk to each other in order to achieve this goal.

- These processes should be linked to other indigenous people's organisations, through **sharing and constructive learning** and the inclusion of women's visions, rights, and participation.

Notes

[1] Guatemalan Commission for Historical Clarification (1999) 'Guatemala Memory of Silence: Report of the Commission for Historical Clarification, Conclusions and Recommendations', http://shr.aaas.org/guatemala/ceh/report/english/toc.html (last accessed September 2008).

[2] According to the Secretary of Planning and Programming for the President (SEGEPLAN). See www.segeplan.gob.gt (last accessed September 2008).

[3] BBC MUNDO.com (2006) 'Guatemala: "sigue la impunidad"' ('Impunity Continues'), 28 May, http://news.bbc.co.uk/hi/spanish/latin_america/newsid_5024000/5024388.stm (last accessed September 2008).

[4] World Health Organization (2007) 'Statistical Report on Violence in Guatemala', www.who.int/violence_injury_prevention/violence/national_activities/gtm/en/index.html (last accessed September 2008).

[5] National Statistics Institute (2006) 'Encuesta Nacional de Condiciones de Vida (ENCOVI) 2006', www.ine.gob.gt/index.php/demografia-y-poblacion/42-demografiaypoblacion/64-encovi2006 (last accessed September 2008).

[6] Inter Press Service (2007) 'Indígenas – Guatemala: Educar a dos voces' ('Indigenous People – Guatemal: Educating in two voices'), November, http://ipsnoticias.net/print.asp?idnews=86728 (last accessed October 2008).

[7] Kaqla' Mayan Women's Group (2000) 'Colours from the Rainbow: Mayan Women's Reality', Guatemala, November.

[8] Guatemalan National Revolutionary Unity (2005) 'Femicides in Guatemala: Crimes against Humanity', Guatemala, November.

[9] Fundación Sobrevivientes (n.d.) 'Analysis of the Situation of Violence Against Women in Guatemala', www.sobrevivientes.org/docs/AnalisisSitMj.pdf (last accessed October 2008).

[10] Oficina de Derechos Humanos del Arzobispado de Guatemala (Archbishop's Office for Human Rights in Guatemala) (2005) 'Décimo Informe: Situación de la Niñez en Guatemala, 2005' ('The 10th Report on the Situation of Childhood in Guatemala'), www.ciprodeni.org/Documentos/Documentos/Informe2005.pdf (last accessed October 2008).

[11] BBC MUNDO.com (2006), op.cit.

[12] A. Hougas (2002) 'Impunity and Building a Peaceful Tomorrow', presentation to the 'Building a Peaceful Tomorrow' Unitarian & Interfaith Conference, Madison, November, www.danenet.org/amnesty/impunitybuildingpeace.html (last accessed September 2008).

[13] World Health Organization (2007), op.cit.

[14] National Commission for Monitoring and Supporting the Strengthening of Justice (2007) 'Indigenous People's Access to the Justice System in Guatemala', Guatemala, May.

[15] Carlos Castresana, Director of the International Commission against Impunity in Guatemala (CICIG), during a public forum in Guatemala City, 5 December 2007.

[16] Guatemalan Institute for Comparative Studies in Penal Sciences (Observatorio de Justicia Penal) (2006) 'Primer Informe', Guatemala. For more information, email iccpg@iccpg.org.gt.

[17] National Commission for Monitoring and Supporting the Strengthening of Justice (2007), *op.cit.*

[18] 'Una mirada desde los pueblos indígenas sobre la aplicación de la Convención Internacional sobre la eliminación de todas las formas de discriminación racial' (An Indigenous Pespective on the Application of the International Convention on the Elimination of all Forms of Racial Discrimination). Informe de Sociedad Civil, Guatemala, presentado al Comité para la Eliminación de la Discriminación Racial de las Naciones Unidas, en ocasión de su 68° periodo de sesiones, febrero de 2006. (A Guatemalan civil-society report presented to the UN Committee on the Elimination of Racial Discrimination in February 2006). For more information, email info@oxfam.org.gt.

[19] Declarations from Alexei Avtonomov, Rapporteur for Guatemala, United Nations Committee for Eliminating Racial Discrimination, 27 February 2006.

[20] Agreement on the Rights and Cultural Identity of Indigenous Peoples, signed between the Guatemalan government and the guerrillas in March 1995.

[21] Guatemalan Commission for Historical Clarification (1999), *op.cit,* 'Chapter II: Genocide Acts'.

[22] Maya Defence Organisation (2006) 'An Experience in the Application and Administration of Indigenous Justice', Guatemala: DEMA.

[23] Co-operants' Exchange Group on Judicial Pluralism in Guatemala, Work Criteria, August 2007.

[24] United Nations (2008) 'Report of the High Commissioner for Human Rights on the Activities of her office in Guatemala', February, (A/HRC/7/38/Add.1), www.ohchr.org/EN/countries/LACRegion/Pages/GTIndex.aspx (last accessed October 2008).

[25] Inter-American Human Rights Tribunal Resolution, 30 May 1997; Human Rights Virtual Library, University of Minnesota.

[26] Inter-American Court for Human Rights, Resolutions: 22 June 1994 and 27 November 1998. Notes from interviews with Defensoria Staff, and direct interview with Fermina López in December 2007.

[27] This section is based on monitoring reports, reports from the Indigenous Defence Organisations, interviews with personnel form these organisations, women beneficiaries, the work of Marta Leticia García Ajucum of Oxfam, and consultant Ada Melgar.

[28] J. Estrada (2007) 'Prevalece impunidad en violencia contra la mujer. Más de 500 feminicidios; 17 mil 560 denuncias de violencia contra la mujer' ('Violence against women continues unpunished. More than 500 femicides; 17,560 accusations of violence against women'), *La Hora*, Guatemala, 23 November, www.lahora.com.gt/hemeroteca.php?fch=2007-11-23 (last accessed October 2008).

[29] Indigenous Women's Defence Office (2007) 'Indigenous Women's Access to the Official Justice System in Guatemala', Guatemala, pp. 25–7.

[30] J. Tuckman (2007) 'They keep on killing and killing', *The Guardian*, April, www.guardian.co.uk/world/2007/apr/20/gender.uk (last accessed September 2008).

[31] *La Cuerda* (2005) 'Penal System Reproduces Gender Discrimination', July; interview with Kenia Reyes, penal system researcher, Guatemala.

[32] Amnesty International (2005) 'Without Protection nor Justice: Women Homicides in Guatemala', June.

[33] *La Prensa Libre* (2007) 'Man murders wife', 1 February; Centre for Informative Reports on Guatemala (2007) 'Population demands justice for murder of their neighbour', 10 May.

[34] International Labour Organisation (n.d.) 'Diversidad lingüística y cultural del pueblo maya y la juventud indígena rural' ('Challenges for an Indigenous Rural Youth Policy in Guatemala'), www-ilo-mirror.cornell.edu/public/spanish/region/ampro/cinterfor/temas/youth/doc/not/libro38/iii/index.htm (last accessed October 2008).

[35] National Statistics Institute (2006), *op.cit.*

[36] Interview with Anastasia Suy by Oxfam GB consultant Ada Melgar.

[37] Interviews with indigenous women attended by Indigenous Defence Organisations and Oxfam GB partners in Guatemala, February to December 2007.

Cover photograph: Oxfam GB

Oxfam GB, November 2008

This paper was written by Mayra Muralles and Rebecca Fries. We acknowledge the assistance of Ada Melgar and Marta Leticia García in its production. Thank you to Nikki van der Gaag who edited the paper and to Emily Laurie who provided research assistance. It is part of a series of papers written to inform public debate on development and humanitarian policy issues. The text may be freely used for the purposes of campaigning, education, and research, provided that the source is acknowledged in full.

For further information please email publish@oxfam.co.uk

Online ISBN 978-1-84814-062-2. This paper is part of a set **Speaking Out: How the voices of poor people are shaping the future** available for purchase from Oxfam Publishing or its agents, print ISBN 978-0-85598-638-4 for the set of 12 papers. For more information visit http://publications.oxfam.org.uk/oxfam/display.asp?ISBN=9780855986384

This paper is also available in French and Spanish.

Oxfam GB

Oxfam GB is a development, relief, and campaigning organisation that works with others to find lasting solutions to poverty and suffering around the world. Oxfam GB is a member of Oxfam International.
Oxfam House
John Smith Drive
Cowley
Oxford
OX4 2JY

Tel: +44.(0)1865.473727
E-mail: enquiries@oxfam.org.uk
www.oxfam.org.uk

8. Get Heard!

People living in poverty in the UK give their views on government policy

Central Liverpool – one of the cities where 'Get Heard' workshops took place

One in five people in the UK lives in poverty. They suffer not just from low incomes, but from discrimination and prejudice. Their voices are rarely heard, especially by those in power. This paper describes a unique experiment to bring the voices of those living in poverty to the attention of the UK government as part of the National Action Plan for Social Inclusion. 'Get Heard' was one of the largest projects of its kind ever undertaken in the UK and is viewed as a model of good practice within the European Union. The paper explains how the project worked, and draws out the lessons learned for the future.

Introduction

The United Kingdom (UK) may be part of the rich world, but one in five people lives in poverty.[1] Many are unable to afford the essentials they need to live a dignified life, such as adequate clothing, sufficient food for their children, or heating for their homes. The UK has the sixth largest economy in the world,[2] and currently ranks 16th on the United Nations Human Development Index, but it is the least equal society in the European Union (EU).[3]

The word 'poverty' has become increasingly used in tandem with the term 'social exclusion'.[4] This helps to focus on how people are affected by low incomes, rather than solely concentrating on the incomes themselves. 'Social exclusion' is used to emphasise the processes which push people to the edge of society, limit their access to resources and opportunities, and curtail their participation in normal social and cultural life.

Each country, influenced by its specific history and culture, creates a structure that puts some citizens at a significant disadvantage. Within the UK, as in other countries, this results in communities or sectors of society who are more vulnerable to the challenges of life. These people include many women, elderly people, migrants, black and minority ethnic people, those who are disabled, and children. For example, one in three children – 3.8 million – are currently living in poverty in the UK, one of the highest rates in the industrialised world.[5] Women are 14 per cent more likely than men to live in households with incomes that are below 60 per cent of the national average.[6] Evidence from the programme indicates that people living in poverty found it difficult, if not impossible, to voice their opinions about what caused and what maintains their poverty. They lack the opportunities, contacts, and links to have a say about the issues affecting their lives. As these people pointed out:

'Being poor and not being able to provide for the child you love can cause depression.'

'We [disabled people] are fed up with the "sit in the corner and be quiet" syndrome.'

'Being in receipt of benefits or on a low wage breeds high-interest debt, isolation, loneliness, low self-esteem.'

'So many people just don't have the *confidence*, they have no *self-worth*. Much of poverty has to do with finance, but there are routes out of poverty that come with confidence.'[7]

In order to reduce poverty and social exclusion, those in power need to listen to people from groups who are socially excluded. In June 2001, EU member states published their first National Action Plans on Social Inclusion (NAPs), opening up a space to let people in poverty have their say about their government's anti-poverty policy approaches. Each EU country must produce a NAP every two years, and participants must include a wide range of groups, from government officials to those living in poverty. In the UK, in 2004, different groups mobilised into a campaign called 'Get Heard' in order to feed into the 2006 NAP.

The Get Heard project: hearing those in poverty

Get Heard was one of the largest projects ever undertaken in the UK where people with first-hand experience of poverty gave their views on government policies designed to combat poverty. The campaign was set up by the Social Policy Task Force (SPTF),[8] a coalition of anti-poverty organisations, and funded by the European Commission, the UK government's Department for Work and Pensions (DWP), Oxfam GB, and the Church of Scotland. There were 2.5 paid posts and many volunteers.

Grassroots community members gave their views through workshops, which they organised themselves, usually with the help of their regional anti-poverty network. A total of 146 workshops were held around the UK between December 2004 and December 2005: 81 in England, 45 in Scotland, 14 in Northern Ireland, and six in Wales. A large number of people took part, from a wide range of different geographical areas and communities of interest, such as: people with experience of mental ill-health; Asian women; single mothers; parents of young children and parents of teenagers; unemployed men; travellers' groups; debt-support groups; domestic violence survivors' groups; asylum seekers and migrants – and many others.

Get Heard workshop participants were asked to talk about government policies and initiatives, and to answer the questions: 'What's working?', 'What's not working?', and 'How should things be done differently?'. The participants selected the topics themselves. The following case study is an example of the opportunities participants felt the project provided for them.

Kenny Brabbins, participant in Merseyside workshop[9]

Kenny lives on government benefits and is about to reach pensionable age. He became involved in Get Heard through a local trust because he believed that: 'people in my age group aren't usually listened to'.

He was pleased and surprised that people listened to him in the workshop; this encouraged his confidence to speak in public. He thinks it is unusual to have such a situation because people in poverty tend to be withdrawn, thinking: 'I don't want to get involved'.

The workshop helped him to build a collective identity with others in poverty: 'I'm not the only one in this situation; we're all the same...I started to get more positive in my attitude...'. Kenny's overview comment shows the empowerment and voice available through the project: 'Get Heard to me personally means that I get heard'.

Now he is encouraging other people from his community to get involved.

The Get Heard project was the first national-level project in a wealthy country to provide people in poverty a platform from which they could speak out and become active participants in their society. Despite encouragement to include all actors, no other EU country had major participation from those in poverty in their NAPs. Get Heard has been well received, and within the EU it is cited as good practice. It is also an example of using successful poverty-reducing techniques from the South, such as Participatory Poverty Assessments (PPAs), and applying them to the North.

Findings

The participants in the Get Heard project were able to choose whatever issues they wanted to cover. The following five were those most frequently discussed, demonstrating the greatest concerns of workshop participants:

1   Perceptions of people experiencing poverty must change.

2   The benefits system must be reformed to really help people experiencing poverty.

3   Parents must be appreciated and better understood.

4   Services must be reformed so that they really work for people experiencing poverty.

5   People experiencing poverty must be involved and listened to.[10]

The majority of these concerns (1, 3, and 5) refer to issues of dignity and power within society. The findings of the project show that people in poverty want more than just more money to spend. They want to be visible, respected members of society.

Of course, economic concerns were also important – the most popular topics were issues relating to work, welfare, benefits, and training. Once in poverty it is incredibly hard to pull yourself out of it, due to the structure of the benefit system. For example, unemployment benefits often end the day before someone starts a new job, but that person will not receive his or her wages until the end of the next month. For someone in poverty it is impossible for them to find the means to live on during that intervening time, which makes it safer to stay on benefits rather than find work. Get Heard showed that people living in poverty must be listened to, not just because it is fair, but because it is the only way to get accurate information on how to best improve policies on reducing poverty.

> **Women's voices**[11]
>
> Women in the Get Heard project who often feel they are not listened to, were able to articulate a range of gender-specific problems:
>
> 'There is still an expectation that women will be compliant, work more and longer for less pay, and do most of the domestic stuff but not take charge. Also that they will be there to support their children irrespective of what the father does.'
>
> 'Successful women are seen as too bossy, but men are praised and given better jobs.'
>
> 'Women get into debt to give their children a better life.'
>
> 'I see the children don't go short but it is all a bit basic. There's nothing spare for luxuries. I shouldn't complain because we aren't terrorised here, we have a roof over our heads and we aren't hungry or cold – most of the time.'
>
> 'No one really knows how little I live on. My neighbours are quite well off and I try to maintain standards. They don't know how mean my ex-husband is. He's a pillar of our community and no one would believe how he treats me. I cannot remember when I could last afford to buy a pair of shoes.'

The impact of the project

The information from the workshops gives the most well-rounded and comprehensive picture of the reality of life for people in poverty in the UK, and how their lives are impacted by government policy. The project had an impact in four main ways: supporting people in poverty to influence policy; demonstrating the importance of participation; supporting the work of other anti-poverty organisations; and encouraging active citizenship.

Supporting people in poverty to influence policy

The findings of Get Heard were submitted to the DWP. The project was part of the NAP 2006 process and has been influential in the planning of NAP 2008. According to Clare Cochrane of Oxfam GB's UK Poverty Programme, 'The NAP process is not an opportunity to lobby for new policy initiatives, but the NAP when published provides a clear guide to government social exclusion policy, and when the process is inclusive of people with experience of poverty, provides an important mechanism for dialogue between government and grassroots on social exclusion policy.'[12] It is problematic to trace direct links from the Get Heard workshops to policy developments, but there have been policy developments that correspond with demands made by workshop participants, and Get Heard undoubtedly raised awareness of such concerns. For example, the Treasury wrote off the debts for tax-credit overpayments, and also changed the tax-credit limit. Both of these ideas were issues frequently discussed and passionately supported in Get Heard workshops.

Demonstrating the importance of participation

The success of the project highlighted the importance of involving poor people in the policy process. The praise Get Heard received from Europe, and the usefulness of the information for policy makers, resulted in the process being a catalyst for further participation projects. For example, the DWP organised a conference in May 2007 on 'Working together to reduce poverty and inequality'. This included people living in poverty discussing the issues highlighted in the Get Heard project. It brought government ministers and policy makers face-to-face with those who are affected by the policies they design.

Supporting the work of anti-poverty organisations

The project helped to increase and improve the anti-poverty network by making its findings available to other organisations. For example, the Migrants Resource Centre in London used the findings of the project to publish a report examining how migrants experience poverty and social exclusion in the UK.[13]

Other organisations have used the project in a number of ways to make sure the voices of people living in poverty are heard by government. For example, a senior citizens' group in East Anglia lobbied local government for better housing; and groups in Merseyside held workshops and wrote a report called 'Merseyside Gets Heard: A Profile of Social Exclusion and Poverty on Merseyside' that they can use to lobby local and regional government.

Encouraging active citizenship

The workshops showed those involved that they are not alone in their situation and that they can influence the government policies affecting them. People were empowered through the respect they received, and the workshops reduced their sense of helplessness and isolation. The project motivated people to move away from the view that: 'There is no chance [for] people like us to make an improvement in our lives',[14] towards a more positive outlook. When people believe they can have an impact, they are more willing to become actively involved in policy-influencing work.

Get Heard will continue to influence poverty and social exclusion policies. This is apparent from the NAP 2006 to 2008 strategy plans. It is often referred to in order to reinforce the points that are being made, for example around low pay; the NAP explains how getting people back into work does not automatically result in them moving out of poverty. Quotes from Get Heard are included to underpin the argument, such as; '[On low pay] you end up working on the same poverty line that you are trying to move on from'.[15]

Get Heard has also influenced the process of the 2008 NAP. The involvement of civil society and people in poverty is now taken as an essential part of the current and future strategy. Although another Get Heard is not planned, a project built on its foundation is emerging. This year, Oxfam will submit a paper on gender and social exclusion to the NAP 2008, as part of the 'Gender Works' project. This will explore the ways in which structural barriers cause and deepen women's social exclusion in three European countries – the UK, Austria, and Italy. The project will involve women in policy processes, build grassroots women's capacity for policy involvement, develop and disseminate tools for gender policy-making, train decision-makers in the use of gendered statistical and methodological tools, and provide gender-awareness training for those involved in tackling social exclusion in these three countries. The project gives a voice to women, and crucially also encourages the gender awareness of those in power.

The Get Heard project has provided a basis on which to build similar work. It has shown that speaking out in this way means that people living in poverty can influence policy and can also gain confidence – and know that their voices are being heard.

Problems and limitations

Get Heard tried to involve as many people as possible in the project, but was not able to access all community groups or all parts of the UK equally. As it was not meant to be a research or policy project there were some limitations to how much it succeeded in opening a space for all people to have their say. The main limitations were: regional variation; lack of involvement of particular groups; and inadequate local-government support.

Regional variations

The workshops were not evenly distributed throughout the UK. For example, 30 per cent took place in Scotland, while only 4 per cent were in Wales. The variations reflected where anti-poverty networks were strong and where they were weak; there is a well-established Poverty Alliance in Scotland that enabled Get Heard to be influential there.

Lack of involvement of particular groups

People only generally got involved in the project when they were part of established networks that were used to meeting and discussing personal topics. Social groupings outside these networks failed to engage with the project. For example, only one group of black men took part (although there were some individuals who took part in other groups), and there were no Asian men involved at all.[16] The other significant group that did not take part was low-paid workers, because they are more reluctant to accept the fact that they are poor, and because workshops were held during the working week.

Lack of local-government support

Though local governments could have been very helpful in facilitating the groups, many failed to show interest in the workshops. They did not see how they would benefit from getting involved in the NAPs. Their increased support and involvement would have helped to ensure that workshops took place, especially where anti-poverty networks were weak.

Recommendations

The Get Heard project had many successful elements; below are some ideas to help improve similar projects in future, including participants' views.

- Increase the lobbying elements of such projects and build this in from the start, so the findings can have a greater influence on policy. This can be done by deepening working relationships and expanding opportunities for dialogue between civil-society organisations (including both community-based organisations and larger NGOs), and government.

- Fund anti-poverty groups in advance to prepare proposals and ensure that they are adequately resourced throughout the process. This is especially important for smaller, grassroots organisations.

- Identify specific hard-to-reach groups, such as women and men from minority ethnic communities, at the beginning of the project. Put in place strategies to reach them through other existing community-based organisations, or through other local-government channels.

- Identify the barriers to working with local government, and the priorities of local authorities, in order to be able to work effectively with them and to use their processes and structures as channels for outreach to low-income community members.

- Ensure that regional variations in the strength of anti-poverty networks are taken into account at the start of a project. Countries with weaker networks could be allocated specific resources to build them up.

- Ensure that there is support and co-ordination between organisations in the network. This is crucial to the success of the project.

- Monitor and evaluate the extent to which bringing policy makers face-to-face with those who are affected influences those policies, and what else has an influence.

- Develop the capacity of anti-poverty networks around the UK to provide a sure foundation and dissemination network for any future participation projects.

Recommendations from participants[17]

Increase the depth of participation.

Follow up with action to show that people consulted are heard. 'It's really important to deliver when you collect people's thoughts and experiences.'

Make participation and consultation meaningful: do not use 'tokenistic participation, where "they hold consultations, but the decisions are already made", resulting in time and work invested by people [being] wasted; consultation needs to be a "two-way process"'.

Mainstream participation in decision-making: extend processes such as those used in Neighbourhood Renewal to other policy making.*

Widen participation: involve a wider range of grassroots community members – think about when and how consultations are held and how stakeholder involvement is invited, and how to enable more marginalised community members to participate.

Increase high-level support for participation and dialogue: MPs should give more support to the All Parliamentary Group on Poverty,** and local authorities should give 'more acknowledgement...that they "work for us"'.

Increase awareness among grassroots and community groups as to how they can influence decision-making locally, and support them to do so.

* Neighbourhood Renewal is the UK government's urban regeneration strategy in England.

** The All Party Parliamentary Group on Poverty is an interest group for Members of Parliament in the House of Commons. They meet regularly to discuss particular poverty issues, and lobby government and raise awareness amongst parliamentarians.

Notes

[1] Oxfam GB, 'UK poverty: how comfortable are you with poverty in the UK?', www.oxfam.org.uk/resources/ukpoverty/index.html (last accessed September 2008). The 'poverty' refered to in this paper is relative poverty, not absolute poverty. Relative poverty equates to people living on incomes which are below 60 per cent of the contemporary median.

[2] In terms of purchasing power parity (PPP).

[3] According to the EU Gini Index, www.eurofound.europa.eu/areas/qualityoflife/eurlife/index.php?template=3&radioindic=158&idDomain=3 (last accessed September 2008).

[4] The Poverty Site, 'Relative poverty, absolute poverty, and social exclusion', www.poverty.org.uk/summary/social%20exclusion.shtml (last accessed September 2008).

[5] See www.endchildpoverty.org.uk/ (last accessed September 2008).

[6] 'Women more likely than men to live in poverty', *The Guardian*, 17 September 2003, www.guardian.co.uk/money/2003/sep/17/womenandmoney.socialexclusion (last accessed September 2008).

[7] Participants in Get Heard workshops. Get Heard (2006) 'People Experiencing Poverty Speak Out on Social Exclusion: National Action Plan on Social Inclusion 2006', www.ukcap.org/getheard/pdf/Get%20 Heard%20report%202nd%20print.pdf (last accessed September 2008).

[8] Including the European Anti-Poverty Network, England; Poverty Alliance, Scotland; Northern Ireland Anti-Poverty Network; Anti-Poverty Network Cymru, Wales; Oxfam's UK Poverty Programme; the UK Coalition Against Poverty; and Age Concern.

[9] Interview with Kim Rowe, Oxfam GB, December 2005.

[10] Get Heard (2006) *op.cit.,* p. 4.

[11] *Ibid.*, p. 30.

[12] Taken from interview with Clare Cochrane.

[13] Migrants Resource Centre (2006) 'A Stronger Voice', www.migrantsresourcecentre.org.uk/index.php?option=com_content&view=article&id=56&Itemid=70 (last accessed September 2008).

[14] Get Heard (2006) *op.cit.*, p. 31.

[15] Department for Work and Pensions (2006) 'UK National Report on Strategies for Social Protection and Social Inclusion: 2006–2008', p.19, www.dwp.gov.uk/publications/dwp/2006/socialprotection/ (last accessed September 2008).

[16] Since the Get Heard project, Oxfam GB has set up a Race Programme, which has established links with these previously excluded groupings.

[17] Get Heard (2006) *op.cit.*, p. 39.

Cover photograph: Karen Robinson/Oxfam 2006

Oxfam GB

Oxfam GB is a development, relief, and campaigning organisation that works with others to find lasting solutions to poverty and suffering around the world. Oxfam GB is a member of Oxfam International.

Oxfam House
John Smith Drive
Cowley
Oxford
OX4 2JY

Tel: +44.(0)1865.473727
E-mail: enquiries@oxfam.org.uk
www.oxfam.org.uk

9. Driving Change

Policies favouring poor people in Indonesia

'Driving Change' partners march for the right to participate in government planning and budgeting processes

This paper shows how the 'Driving Change' project in Indonesia used advocacy and capacity-building to ensure that the voices of poor people, especially women, became part of government planning processes to alleviate poverty. It focuses on people's participation at village level as a key entry point, leading to advocacy for policy change at district and national levels. It also shows the successes and challenges of this kind of work for pro-poor policy development, and the need for deeper participatory approaches on poverty reduction.

Introduction

Indonesia has come a long way since the 1998 Asian financial crisis drove many millions of people into poverty. It has moved from low-income to middle-income status. It is now 107th out of 177 in the United Nations Human Development Index,[1] and is progressing well towards its 2015 Millennium Development Goals. It has also undergone some major social and political changes – the World Bank notes that it is: 'emerging as a vibrant democracy with decentralised government and far greater social openness and debate.'[2] The current government has been in power since 2004.

However, one authority notes that: 'For the large population of poor, especially urban poor and landless farmers, social and economic rights are compromised and opportunities for control over key aspects of their own welfare are severely restricted.'[3] Today, more than 55 per cent of the population (115 million people) live on less than $2 per day. Many more remain vulnerable to poverty, or lack access to crucial services such as health and education. There are also huge disparities between regions, with areas of eastern Indonesia being poorer. In addition:

- Twenty-five per cent of children below the age of five are malnourished.

- The maternal mortality rate in 2005 was 420 deaths of mothers in every 100,000 births, which is much worse than that of other comparable countries in the region – the figure for Viet Nam was 150, and for Thailand 100.[4]

- Fifty-five per cent of the poorest fifth of the population do not complete junior secondary school, compared with 89 per cent of the richest fifth.[5]

- Only 48 per cent of the poorest people living in rural areas have access to safe water and less than 1 per cent of them have access to piped sewerage services.[6]

Findings from seven districts identified government policies as a major cause of regional poverty.[7] Initiatives to improve food security, education, and environmental sustainability are slow, and poverty initiatives are not being carried out at local and district levels, despite a process of decentralisation. This is partly due to a skills shortage among staff at these levels, and partly due to government cuts which resulted in a real reduction in the support provided by the state to marginalised and excluded populations, especially in the fields of education and health. In addition, lack of public participation in the design and implementation of government policies, particularly by civil-society organisations (CSOs), makes those policies less effective in tackling poverty.

Research revealed four major problems with government policy formation and implementation around anti-poverty issues:[8]

1 Government development plans at both local and central levels are not based on an analysis of poverty. Policies and plans more commonly reflect the interests of institutions and agents within state institutions than the interests of poor and vulnerable people.

2 There is a disjuncture between planning and budget-monitoring processes. Decisions about budget allocations are often not linked to any assessment of the performance of local government in terms of improving the lives of poor people. As a result, local governments which do not perform well continue to be funded.

3 There is little transparency and accountability in planning, decision-making, or resource flows targeted at poverty reduction by government and institutional donors.

4 Civil society and community-level organisations are largely marginalised in the process through which development interventions are designed, implemented, and assessed.

The 'Driving Change' project

The 'Driving Change' project was set up by Oxfam to address some of these problems. It aimed to reduce poverty, improve access for poor people to quality services, and reduce gender disparities. Using Participatory Poverty Assessments (PPAs) and other tools, the project worked with local CSOs and poor and vulnerable community members to improve their skills in engaging with decision-makers. It aimed not just to make it easier for poor people to negotiate with those in power, but also to give them their own say in how negotiations take place.

Funded by the British government's Department for International Development (DFID), Driving Change was based in four provinces: South Sulawesi, South-East Sulawesi, East Nusa Tenggara, and East Java (Island of Madura), combined with national-level activities in the capital city, Jakarta. The four provinces were selected because they were considered the most vulnerable on a number of measures in relation to human development, poverty, and gender.

The project, which ran between April 2005 and April 2008, was implemented with six NGO partners at local levels (district and village) and through one partner at national level.[9] The role of the implementing partners was to organise the communities and to engage them in government planning, monitoring, and evaluation of pro-poor policies. The project targeted poor people and those vulnerable to poverty, according to criteria set by the Indonesian government.[10] It reached a total of almost four million: 1,412,100 poor people and 2,294,863 vulnerable people.

Building capacity – Participatory Poverty Assessments

Driving Change saw capacity-building as one of the best ways of engaging key stakeholders, including the government, local network partners, and local communities. Capacity-building of local partners included a range of methodologies and skills development, such as gender mainstreaming, advocacy work, and financial management, as well as community organising, Participatory Poverty Assessments (PPAs), policy reviews, and participatory monitoring and evaluation.

Participatory Poverty Assessments

A Participatory Poverty Assessment is a process for including poor people's views in the analysis of poverty and in the design of strategies to reduce it.

A PPA starts from the point of view of poor and very poor people, giving voice to their concerns and in this way counter-balancing the top-down approach of most policy thinking. It also provides a set of local case studies – rich in contextual detail that emphasises the multi-dimensionality of poverty and the complexity and dynamics of local coping and adapting strategies. This complements the information from other poverty-related surveys. The combination of statistical information and voices from a PPA provides a good basis for innovative thinking about reducing poverty.[11]

PPAs were the main tool and organising framework of the project. They provided a platform and opportunity for poor people, both women and men, to analyse the local situation with regard to poverty. They also 'mapped' the social context in relation to the rights of poor people, and prepared advocacy strategies and action plans. They helped to:

1   identify drivers of poverty that are specific to local contexts, relevant given the diversity of the project areas; and

2   strengthen the credibility of local NGO partners and ensure that their interventions are increasingly evidence-based.

However, since partners were often faced with a range of issues that emerged from the PPA exercises, they found it difficult to identify intervention strategies where they could have an impact. In response, Oxfam supported partners by facilitating partner-specific advocacy assessments. The aim of the assessments was primarily to survey the external context in which partners were operating in order to identify opportunities for engaging with government and influencing local policies and practices. The findings of the advocacy assessments, paired with the PPA findings, helped shape what partners decided to do next.

This work increased the ability of civil society to learn from, and work with, poor people, especially on the issues of basic rights and gender. Saleh, Programme Officer of FIKORNOP (Forum Informasi dan komunikasi Organisasi Non Pemerintah Sulawesi Selatan), a Driving Change partner, said: 'Though working with poor communities was not new for us, in the Driving Change project we gained a new experience working with Participatory Poverty Assessments (PPAs). The PPA not only helped to fight for the rights of the poor, but also helped us to develop new, fairer, social relationships. We first thought that the advocacy using PPA would be soft, but in fact, we realized that it has a strong message, because it involves working with a clear methodology and finding out facts with the poor about their poverty issues'.

Strengthening the voices of poor people and women in local forums

There are many factors that prevent poor people, especially women, from participating in Indonesian society, and especially in forums where decisions are taken. Indonesia is a patriarchal society dominated by strong religious and cultural norms, and with fixed views about women and their social status. This also extends to poor people, who are not seen as capable of participating in government or society.

These views stem from a number of other beliefs – that government is the work of bureaucrats and politicians and not of the people; that only educated people can contribute and talk in public forums; that women's place is in the home; that men's role is to represent women; and that poor people cannot become leaders. This is also true of the *musrenbangs*,[12] which have a traditional leader; village leaders; spiritual leaders; teachers; and landlords – all of whom are men with status in the community.

The *musrenbangs*

Poor people and women normally have few possibilities for participating in the *musrenbangs*. It is not surprising then that the need to participate in *musrenbangs* was seen by many Driving Change participants as the most important opportunity for poor people to make their voices heard and to influence pro-poor planning and budgeting.

As a result of the project, *musrenbangs* began to be seen as effective forums for poor people, especially poor women, to participate in. Their proposals began to be included in planning and budget allocations. For example, with the help of Yayasan Pengembangan Studi Hukum dan Kebijakan (YPSHK), a Driving Change partner, farmers in Wawombalata were given a sprayer machine and a well-drilling machine; the rubbish-collection community received an incinerator for waste treatment; and fisher people in Petoaha, a fish stall. The struggle of the Nanga-Nanga people, who fought for land certification, is another successful example.

Nanga-Nanga's dreams

In 1965, more than a million people were killed and many more sent to jail without any legal process in the name of fighting 'communism'. Nanga-Nanga today is an isolated village of 52 families of these ex-political prisoners. The road that connects the village to the nearest town was only laid two years back. Road construction is still not completed; it is dusty and bumpy in dry seasons, and muddy and wet in the rainy seasons. There is no electricity.

The families survived by trying to nurture the infertile land, which did not belong to them, but which they dreamed of owning. But this presented a problem, says Aco, the representative of local NGO YPSHK. 'On one side they want to develop the land's agriculture potential and harvest maximum crop, on other side they are afraid if they produce too much, the land will be snatched by the private landowner or the government'.

In May 2006, with the support of Driving Change, an organisation was formed in Nanga-Nanga to campaign for ownership of the land. It was called *Permin*, the Union of the Nanga-Nanga Community.

After a relatively short time, Resman, the vice-chair of this organisation, was optimistic about gaining official ownership of the land: 'the government has promised to give us the land certificate over 20 hectares for each family. We will wait!' By 2008, around 20 families had received land certification. The inhabitants of Nanga-Nanga now have reason to believe their dream will become a reality.

Oxfam Newsletter ARAH, Makassar

Women were able to raise issues in the *musrenbang* and ensure their access to public services such as education, health, natural resources, and economic services. In Rakateda 1 village, for example, 80 per cent of women's proposals at the village-level *musrenbang* were given planning priority. These proposals were seen to meet not only women's needs, but those of children and men as well. They included proposals for a local child-care centre, environmental sanitation, and technical assistance to agricultural extension workers. Mrs Genoveva, from Flores village, said that they used to produce only one bag of soya beans every six months, which became 2.5 bags after technical guidance from the agricultural extension worker who had been approved as a result of women's participation in the *musrenbang*.

Darmawati Daeng Kobo, a woman from Bontokassi-Takalar district, said: 'During the Driving Change project, I became aware; before, our image and voice was buried. Our voice was never heard because we are poor. In this project, I came forward, I attended meetings, we formed a group and presented ourselves everywhere, we went to the village government office, to the district government secretary office, Village Community Empowerment office, Department of Trade and Industry'.

Several groups of women managed to change the traditional structure of marketing; for example a group of craftswomen in Takalar district gradually broke the *papalele* structure of middlemen and women, and sold their work directly.

> **Takalar craftswomen: courage is the real capital**
>
> In Takalar District, craftsmen and craftswomen get credit from a *papalele* (middleman or woman). The *papalele*, being economically stronger, has access to capital. He or she takes loans from the bank and provides these to the craftspeople, either in the form of money or raw materials. Once the product is ready, the *papalele* purchases it from the craftsmen or craftswomen at a rate the *papalele* decides, and sells it in the market, earning more profit.
>
> The Driving Change project enabled craftswomen, who previously used to work individually, to form groups and build their access to institutional credit and the market. In this way, women could take control of their own products from production to marketing. It broke the traditional *papalele* structure. Darmawati Daeng Kobo of Bontokassi, a member of a craftswomen's group, said: 'There is a *papalele* who always collected *songkok* [a hat used while praying] from craftspeople. He became angry with me. He said I created competition with him. He became afraid because he thought I would cause negative impact in his business. I go everywhere, I know the market now. I took products from my group, participated in an exhibition and displayed the products there. My real capital is not money but courage'.
>
> Oxfam Newsletter ARAH, Makassar

However, substantial challenges remain. First, it is still not clear how the *musrenbang* mechanism can be improved to include poor people and women as a matter of course. Second, because the *musrenbang* is only representative of district, sub-district, and municipal levels, it limits the rights of poor people to participate at higher level. Finally, information concerning the *musrenbang* process often does not reach poor communities in the first place.

Changing gender roles

Changing the social roles of women and men is also about changing individual attitudes and prejudices. The presence of a village head who supports gender equality in the village can have more effect than just lobbying by the women themselves. Frans Laja, a village head in Rakateda 1 village, is one such man.

> **Frans Laja: being the change**
>
> Frans Laja, a village head who took part in the capacity-building activities in the Driving Change project, clearly articulated the relationship between gender equality and poverty alleviation: 'Not only do we have to discuss the issue of equality between the sexes, but we have to put it into practice too', he said.
>
> According to Laja, poverty alleviation must start in the family by reducing the woman's burden. He added: 'The reluctance of men to work is mainly

caused by a number of taboos. In the past, it was a taboo for a man to fetch water. Around five to ten years ago, it was still taboo. Now the situation is changing. A respectable man is the one who can fetch water, cradle a baby, and carry the food for pigs, and firewood'.

By his own behaviour, Frans Laja has influenced the men of his village to willingly share the household tasks with their wives. He said: 'I sweep the floor in my house, including the veranda. I want to show my people that the village head can also do household chores. Once I went home from the farm with my wife, carrying the firewood and the pig. The village elders were afraid to give any comment since they knew that I would reply by asking them why they didn't just help carrying the burdens in their own house too'.

Roni, the head of the Flores Institute for Research Development (FIRD), a Driving Change partner, said: 'Frans Laja persuades other communities to change their perceptions of roles of men and women, particularly while participating in various meetings'.

Oxfam Newsletter ARAH, Makassar

As a result of the Driving Change project, women gained more confidence in their relationships with men and became capable of raising their voice about their rights. This began to make a difference even at an institutional level. For example, one Driving Change partner, Pedagang Kaki Lima (PKL), a traditional forum of small vendors, made violence against women an offence, the punishment for which was that the offender had to give up membership.

The positive changes that happened to women also happened to men, who became more aware of power gaps, which led to increased trust between spouses, and more equal roles in the home. However, this change didn't happen universally, and sometimes women felt that not only were they burdened by their domestic role, but now had to find time for a more public role as well.

Making local governments accountable

Through the process of PPAs, communities became more engaged, and this paved the way for a second stage of policy influencing. Driving Change partners built relationships not only with poor communities, but also with policy makers at district, city, and village levels, and in government departments. This created an opportunity for poor people and civil society to help formulate local poverty-reduction strategies, which previously had been dominated by the government and other groups such as business people, donor agencies, academics, and social workers.

People's participation in these local planning processes meant that they were able to influence the development of various policies affecting them. In the targeted districts, local government gave more benefits to poor people in terms of their rights to identity and protection. For example, the rubbish-picking communities who came from rural areas ten years ago and started living on the periphery of the city were not recognised as legal residents. They did not have identity cards, and could not have access to basic services like education, health, and clean water. As a result of the project, community members organised collectively to lobby the municipal government, and they succeeded in getting citizenship cards. They also lobbied for clean piped water, which was funded by a block grant from the district-level government. These successes led to the formation of a network that continues to advocate for their rights.

Mothers too were able to lobby for the changes they wanted in their children's schools. Mrs Ernie, of Kampung Sakura, Makassar city, said: 'before we organised ourselves in a community group, we didn't have the confidence to go to school or talk to the teacher. We felt too timid to go to the sub-district to talk to government officials. However, with the support of Driving Change, we formed an organisation and got confidence to meet with teachers, to go to the village head's office and talk to officials from the education department. I can't believe it happened!'[13]

Overall, there was a major shift from a charitable approach, which had traditionally been the mindset of policy makers and poor people alike, to one in which poor people and women began to feel they had a right to have a say and to demand improvements for their groups and communities.

Lessons learned and recommendations

The Driving Change project showed how work on policy and advocacy has the potential to bring about changes in the lives of poor and vulnerable people, especially women. There are many positive experiences to share, as well as a number of challenges:

1   Community-based advocacy, an integrated approach of community empowerment with rights-based actions, proved successful in allowing the voices of the poorest people to be articulated and heard in decision-making forums, and this led to real changes.

2   Capacity-building of local-level organisations plays an important role in achieving the desired impact. In particular, PPAs helped and supported all stakeholders, including poor people and women, to understand the drivers of poverty and develop strategies for advocacy. PPAs increased communities' capacity to identify and ask for what they needed to improve their lives.

3   The project was a good experience in building collective consensus against poverty. It is a model of how to influence decision-makers to change social and political relationships. The planning and operational process was agreed between the Indonesian partners, Oxfam, and the funder, DFID. More

effective vertical and horizontal links are needed to share experiences and learning.

4   As different partners are effective in different contexts and environments, it is important for them to find ways of working together in order to ensure that their actions are sustainable. The quarterly partnership co-ordination meeting planned in the Driving Change project needed to be supported by other mechanisms such as internal exchange visits, formation of thematic groups, more frequent theme-based meetings, and increased communication through newsletters.

5   Advocacy and networking with grassroots community-based organisations (CBOs) encourages policy change and puts pressure on the government to be accountable by responding to the demands of poor and marginalised communities. The CBOs engaged with district-level governments and strategic forums for poverty reduction, as well as forums at village level (*musrenbangs*). They used a combination of confrontation and collaborative advocacy processes and approaches. These resulted in the government responding to many of the demands from women and the most vulnerable groups.

6   Institutionalising the participation of poor people and women as part of government structures remains a challenge. Driving Change partners tried a dual strategy of influencing reform-minded individuals, and formulating or revising policy regulations. They found that regular follow-up action was needed to consolidate learning, and forward planning in order to institutionalise change.

7   Gender issues gained a higher profile among partners and in local government. The advocacy and governance work through the Driving Change project provides considerable evidence of the impact of gender mainstreaming. This work needs to be carried out in ways that are both more systematic and more shared between partners, so that those with less experience can learn from those with more. Men as well as women need to be involved for change to take place.

8   The project linked various strategies, from PPAs at grassroots level, and village *musrenbangs*, to the strategic forums for poverty reduction at district level. These were used as a means of putting poor people in a position to propose policies based on their own needs and desires.

9   *Musrenbang* village forums still need to find ways of implementing their decisions at higher levels and publicising what they do in the community.

10 Oxfam internal learning processes helped in looking at the ways in which the work on policy advocacy and governance is done. It

was clear that a strong national-level presence is needed to work in this sector. While change at local level is important, it needs to be linked to changes at national level.

The Driving Change project demonstrated strong evidence of the impact of advocacy on pro-poor policy change. In all, Driving Change worked on 42 policies across village, district, and provincial levels. It laid a strong foundation for the pro-poor movement in Indonesia. An impact assessment was carried out towards the end of the project and options are being worked out for sharing the ideas and lessons learned with a wider audience. Drawing on the lessons from this project, it will be possible to build a new kind of governance; one that respects the rights of communities, particularly poor people and women.

Notes

[1] UNDP (2007/8) 'Human Development Report 2007/8', New York: UNDP.

[2] World Bank (2006) 'Making the New Indonesia Work for the Poor – Overview', Washington DC: World Bank.

[3] J. McGrory (2008) 'Indonesia guide', Oneworld.net, http://uk.oneworld.net/guides/indonesia/development (last accessed September 2008).

[4] UNDP (2007/8), *op.cit.*

[5] World Bank (2006), *op.cit.*

[6] *Ibid.*

[7] Through Participatory Poverty Assessments (PPAs).

[8] For the Driving Change project.

[9] The partners were: FIK-ORNOP (Forum Informasi dan Komunikasi Organisasi Non Pemerintah Sulawesi Selatan), YPSHK (Yayasan Pengembangan Study Hukum dan Kebijakan), JPKP (Jaringan Pengembangan Kawasan Pesisir Buton), PIAR (Association of Initiative Developing and People Advocacy), FIRD (Flores Institute for Regional Development), YMM (LSM Madura Mandiri), and Sekretariat GAPRI (Anti-impoverishment Movement of Indonesian People).

[10] Poor people are defined by the government as those who earn below IDR 130,499 a month in urban areas (municipalities) and IDR 96,512 a month in rural areas (districts). Vulnerable people are defined as those who earn 10–18 per cent more than the poverty line defined in the 'Statistics Indonesia' (Central Bureau), www.bps.go.id/ (last checked September 2008), and UNDP (2004) 'Human Development Report 2004', New York: UNDP.

[11] Government of Balochistan (2003) 'Between Hope & Despair: Pakistan Participatory Poverty Assessment', Balochistan report, www.dfid.gov.uk/Pubs/files/ppa-balochistan.pdf (last accessed September 2008).

[12] A *musrenbang* is an annual village-level development-planning process, where local people participate, and their aspirations and needs are presented through submitting proposals to the government.

[13] Focus-group discussion by Driving Change.

Cover photograph: Muhari/Oxfam GB (2007)

Oxfam GB

Oxfam GB is a development, relief, and campaigning organisation that works with others to find lasting solutions to poverty and suffering around the world. Oxfam GB is a member of Oxfam International.

Oxfam House
John Smith Drive
Cowley
Oxford
OX4 2JY

Tel: +44.(0)1865.473727
E-mail: enquiries@oxfam.org.uk
www.oxfam.org.uk

Programme Insights

10. What's in a Name?

Changing policies and beliefs in favour of women in Peru

Demonstration in Peru for the 'Right to a Name' campaign

Millions of people around the world cannot open a bank account, obtain credit, vote, own or inherit property, get a job or a passport, access health care, or sometimes even go to school. The reason? Because they do not have a birth certificate. Until recently, thousands of babies born to single mothers in Peru were denied the right to a name because they were not registered by both their parents. This paper shows how the Alliance for Citizen Rights, a network of non-government organisations, public organisations, women's groups, childhood organisations, academics, and politicians, worked together to change the law and challenge deeply held prejudices against women.

Introduction

Most people do not think about their birth certificate until they need it for a passport or other official document. And yet, without one, you cannot open a bank account, access credit or health care, own or inherit property, vote, find employment, or sometimes even go to school. Birth registration also helps to prevent child labour, and protects girls from early marriage and boys from under-age conscription, as without proof of when you were born you may not know how old you are.

Having your birth registered is a fundamental record of a person's right to exist, enshrined in human-rights declarations like the Convention on the Rights of the Child. South Africa's Archbishop Desmond Tutu said: 'It's time we made this one of the priority concerns of the international community.'[1]

Despite this, more than half of all babies are not registered. This amounts to 51 million people who do not have a record of their right to exist.[2] UNICEF, the United Nations Children's Fund, notes that: 'These unregistered children are almost always from poor, marginalised or displaced families or from countries where systems of registration are not in place or functional.'[3] South Asia has the largest number of unregistered children, with almost 23 million births not registered in 2006.

Number of annual births not registered, by region, 2006[4]

	Millions	Percentage under 5 not registered, 1987–2006[5]
South Asia	22.6	66
Sub-Saharan Africa	19.7	59
East Asia and Pacific	5.1	17
Middle East/North Africa	1.5	16
Latin America/Caribbean	1.1	10
CEE/CIS	0.6	10
Industrialised countries	0.2	2

In Latin America, 1.1 million of the region's 11 million births each year are not registered.[6] At the region's first Conference on Birth Registration and the Right to Identity in 2007, Paraguay's Minister of Justice and Employment, Dr Derlis Céspedes Aguilera, explained the importance of birth registration:

10. What's in a Name?, Speaking Out, Programme Insights, Oxfam GB. November 2008

'When children are not registered...they are denied the identity of a nation and their rights. Not having an identity, the child is exposed to many forms of abuse and exploitation. Guaranteeing their identity allows them to access education, and also to become legal citizens with full rights to public office, education and financial well-being.'[7]

There are many reasons why parents do not register their babies – distance (if they live in a remote area), lack of information, and illiteracy may all contribute. This paper looks at a specific case, that of single mothers in Peru, who did not register their babies because the right to a name and to have a birth certificate depended on proof of the relationship between the father and the mother, and on the presence of the father for the signing of the birth certificate.

This paper shows how these single mothers in Peru were able to campaign to get the law, which discriminated against them and their babies, changed, and at the same time successfully challenge deeply held prejudices against women.

The situation in Peru

Most of those who do not register their babies at birth are either poor, or indigenous, or both. Forty per cent of Peruvians live in poverty. However, in rural areas the poverty rate soars to 75 per cent. Indigenous people make up 40 per cent of the total population and are often also poor.[8]

While Peru is a middle-income country, it has high levels of inequality. The country ranks 87th out of 177 countries in the Human Development Index, with 12 per cent of the population living below the poverty line in 2007.[9] The richest 20 per cent of the population own 55.2 per cent of the country's income, while the poorest 20 per cent own only 3.8 per cent.[10]

Each year, around 110,000 babies are not registered at birth. It is likely that the overall numbers without birth certificates are much higher: in 2006, out of a total population of 27.3 million, 3.5 million did not have identity documents.[11] Parents who do not have birth certificates themselves cannot register their children, who then are more likely to remain in poverty, and so the cycle continues. These people are denied many of the rights to which they are entitled in the country's Constitution.

There are two groups of people who are particularly affected. The first is poor people in rural areas, who were the main victims of the internal armed conflict between 1980 and 2000. The second group, the subject of this paper, are the children of single mothers. Thus those with the least voice and power in society are those whose children are most likely to be denied the right to a name.

Discrimination against women

Women in Peru face discrimination on a number of fronts. For example, they are still under-represented in politics, despite a 1997 law requiring a 30 per cent quota of women candidates in political parties; they earn on average 46 per cent less than men and usually work in less secure occupations; sexual harassment does not qualify as an offence; and illiteracy rates for women are more than double the rates for men.

> **Cooking, washing, ironing...**
>
> The following quote, from Dominica, a rural woman in Peru, giving advice to her son about what he should look for in a wife, highlights the place women hold in Peruvian society:
>
> 'Cooking, washing and ironing, this, young man, this is the life for a woman now. When you look for a wife you're not only going to look for someone for the bed, you have to look for someone to iron, to wash, to make sure they can sew. Although you might not wear knitted socks now, she's going to have to mend your trousers when you get a hole, she's going to do the ironing. This is the work of a woman right till the end.'[12]

Children born to single mothers

The law on birth registration effectively discriminated in particular against the children of women who were single mothers. In Peru, a person must have two surnames: their father's first surname and their mother's first surname. Under the Peruvian Civil Code, the children of married parents automatically have their father's first surname and their mother's first surname.

A married woman can go to a civil registry office with a marriage certificate and the registrar will register the newborn child with the first surname of the spouse on the certificate, followed by her own first surname.

However, until recently, children born outside wedlock were given both surnames only if the father recognised them as his children. This was a problem, as fathers were not always willing to recognise children who were the product of an extra-marital relationship. Norma Rojas, member of the Alliance for Citizen Rights, explained: 'The act of registering does not mean recognition unless both mother and father sign the birth certificate'.[13]

Single mothers were not able to go to a civil registry office, register a child as theirs, and declare the name of the father so that the child could be registered with its father's and mother's first surnames. If the father failed to go to the civil registry office to recognise the child as his, a very common occurrence, the child had to have both of the mother's surnames instead. On the surface, this apparently solved the problem, giving the children of single mothers two surnames as required by Peruvian law.

> **Child of married couple**
>
> María Rodríguez Santos + Silvio Cueto Lopez = Rosa Cueto Rodriguez
>
> **Child of single mother**
>
> Dolores Delgado De Sousa = Alejandro Delgado De Sousa

However, this meant that children born to single mothers appeared to be their siblings rather than their children, since they had the same paternal and maternal surnames as their mother. This situation immediately identified them as children who were not recognised by their fathers, or as the child of an unmarried woman. In a society as conservative as Peru, this was likely to lead to teasing by their peers and to discrimination.

In other cases, the second surname was simply registered as a blank.

> **'My true identity is a blank line'**
>
> Angela Bazán is now an adult who was registered only by her mother. Her father never recognised her, and her identity card still says:
>
> Name: Angela
> First surname: Bazán
> Last surname: _____.
>
> Angela says: 'I do not have an identity, what is my name? I am Angela Bazán plus a line. This is my true identity: a line'.

In order to avoid this stigma, single mothers often preferred not to register their child, in the hope that they could eventually persuade the father to agree to sign the birth certificate. Like the children of poor and indigenous people, such children had no legal existence because they did not officially appear on any legal documents.

The only other option was for the mother to file a paternity suit, which involved going to court, incurring high legal costs, and exposing both her child and herself to a public process where their honour and dignity could be called into question. DNA testing is an option for single mothers in other countries, but this involves finding the father and securing his agreement to be tested. In addition, it is expensive, and unless the state pays, generally the mother cannot afford it. Therefore although the problem of identity is an issue for all single mothers, it affects poor single mothers even more profoundly because without financial resources, they do not have the option to try to resolve the situation using the legal process.

'He has his daddy's eyes, but not his surname'

In June 2004, the Allianza por el Derecho Cuidadano (ADC – 'Alliance for Citizen Rights') was formed in response to widespread concern about this whole issue. The Alliance is made up of more than 15 institutions from civil society, the state, and international agencies, and at the time it was supported by Oxfam GB. Its aim was to use a rights-based approach to address the issue of lack of documentation and to campaign for a change in the law so that a birth certificate did not require the participation of the father as well as the mother. The campaign was entitled: *Tiene los ojos de Papá, pero no su apellido* ('He has his daddy's eyes, but not his surname').

ADC identified the fact that it was Article 321 of the Peruvian Civil Code that prevented single women from registering their children with the surnames of both the father and mother unless both parents went to the civil registry office. Since this was a legal issue, ADC commissioned studies from experts in civil and family law as well as international human-rights law, which gave the campaign a sound legal basis.

ADC sought to demonstrate that the right to a name is a public as well as a private matter, because it is a human right protected by international regulations approved by Peru. This was a new way of looking at civil rights. ADC pointed out that: 'The State must guarantee the right of all Peruvians to an identity and a name and that Peruvians, in turn, have the right to demand that this right be respected'.[14]

Once the results of the studies were obtained, ADC drew up a legal proposal to eliminate Article 321 from the Civil Code, so that a single mother could go to a civil registry office and register her child with the father's surname even when he was not present. She would have the right to mention the name of the father and the civil registrar would be obliged to register the child with the father's first surname (mentioned by the mother) and the mother's first surname. As a result, the child would have its two surnames, just like children born to married parents.

The ADC proposal sought to guarantee the right of all children to a name, regardless of whether the parents were married or not. It was not about paternal obligations, which are only established once the father personally and voluntarily recognises his child. That is a separate issue which has still not been resolved.

Cultural barriers: a father's honour or a child's right?

Discussions in Congress revealed interesting lessons for those who work for a gendered approach to public policies. Members of Congress from all political parties put up strong resistance to changing the current legislation. The most frequent opposing argument was that single women could provide false information about the name of the child's father. Members of Congress pointed out that their duty was to preserve the 'honour' of families constituted by marriage and to protect the 'honour' of men who could be involved in situations affecting their privacy and dignity. They must also protect those wives who could find their marriage and the reputation of their spouses questioned, based on the statements of a single woman who was seeking to attribute the paternity of her 'extra-marital' child.

Antero Flores Araoz, Congressman in the previous government, said: 'The mother can simply say of the father – or the supposed father: "My son is his". How easy! A woman could simply say that such and such a child is the son of Martin Luther King or Bill Clinton, or whoever she wants'. Interestingly, such are the deeply held prejudices against women that some of the mothers from women's organisations in poor neighbourhoods had the same reaction as the members of Congress. Some said: 'But I am a mother, and I wouldn't like some woman saying that my son was the father of a child of hers', or: 'Some women lie, and that is a real risk'.

However, making a false statement to a public official is considered a crime and therefore a false declaration on the part of a single mother would not enjoy impunity under the law, a fact which made it obvious that the resistance was not legal but cultural. Women who are single mothers do not want their children to have the surname of someone who is not their real father; on the contrary, they want the 'real' father to recognise his child and assume all the obligations that a father should legally fulfil: food, education, health, and care, among others. Declaring a false name is, therefore, a strategy that does not work for the mother or the child.

In addition, a series of studies and reports issued by feminist organisations, pro-child organisations, magistrates, and civil registries reported that women who are single mothers do provide the true name of the father of their children. While many men refuse to recognise their children legally, at a social and family level they already tacitly recognise that they are the father.

ADC's strongest legal argument was that where rights conflict, the legislator must opt for that which protects a greater good. In the case of children, the superior interest of the child (the guiding principle of international law regarding children's human rights) and the principle of non-discrimination made it valid to guarantee the child's right to a name, even given the possible, but unlikely, effect it could have on the reputation of adult men.

Press coverage

Interestingly, the press coverage focused on children and the consequences of not being registered, rather than on the plight of single mothers. In the words of one journalist, this was for very practical reasons: 'gender discrimination doesn't sell, children do'. The media used testimonies from children who, because they only had their mother's surnames (even though they might know their father), felt deeply that their name exposed them to society as rejected, unloved beings. They felt they were inferior to children born to a family protected by the state and the law: a family based on marriage. The discussion was not about the right to a name, but rather how the state could guarantee this right by attributing value to a statement made by a single mother.

It became very clear that the reactions of politicians, the press, and even some of the women themselves, were underpinned by very strong cultural barriers which prevent women from identifying the way in which public policies exclude them from exercising their rights. Such is the strength of these barriers and prejudices that talking about rights and gender discrimination is no easy task, even with those who suffer from gender discrimination themselves.

A battle won: linking civil society with the state

One of the strategies used by ADC was to make links between civil society and sympathetic members of government. This gave the campaign legitimacy in the eyes of potential opponents and of the press, who could not argue that this was a campaign of 'opposition' to one state sector or another.

The Ministry of Women and Social Development, an ADC member, and the Minister in particular, played an important role in the campaign. Thanks to ADC, the Minister sent a communication to Congress, attaching the proposal to modify the Civil Code. That proposal was then sent to the Commission for Women and Social Development, chaired by a representative of the governing party.

After months of intense activity in Congress, including several public audiences promoted by ADC, meetings with parliamentary groups, and with members of Congress who are opinion leaders, the modification to the law was put on the Congressional agenda to be debated by 120 members of Congress.

A week before the decisive debate in Congress in March 2006, ADC launched a mass media campaign. A journalist was hired and for two weeks ADC was present on national television and in the written press. The Ministry of Women and Social Development made specific statements referring to ADC and the legislative proposal. At the same time, the member of Congress who was leading the issue on the Women's Commission gave a number of interviews.

Finally, on 30 March 2006, the day of the debate, one of Peru's most important political magazines, *La República*, published a note addressed to Congress encouraging them to vote for the modification. Outside the Congress building where the debate was being held, women from grassroots organisations demonstrated by pretending to 'wash' birth certificates – imitating the 'flag-washing' campaign in 1999, which had contributed to the return of democracy and the resignation of President Alberto Fujimori. Flag-washing symbolised the need to get rid of corruption. 'Washing' the birth certificates highlighted the need to 'clean up' the unequal state of birth registration.

The demonstration was transmitted live from outside the Congress building and attracted considerable media attention.

The amendment to the law was passed by a small Congressional majority. The president, who had to ratify it, subsequently also approved it. ADC and its supporters had managed to modify Peru's Civil Code. As a result children who are born out of wedlock can now have the last name of both parents, just like children born to married couples.

This law thus achieved a change in policy and national legislation. It also demonstrated a change in the practices of policy makers. Confronted with compelling legal arguments, they had to admit that the main arguments against a change that would benefit thousands of children were in fact grounded in prejudice.

It is because of this law, achieved by ADC's campaign, that poor women and their children can now be recognised by the state, and the children can exercise their right to a name and identity, and eliminate the discrimination made by the conservative sector of Peruvian society. Now, the children of single mothers have a name, just as the children of married woman do.

Keys to success

ADC and the Oxfam GB Peru programme offer this experience as a successful example of joint action between the state and civil society to change a law that discriminated against women. This alliance helped to bring about changes in public policies against a backdrop of deeply rooted beliefs about the inferiority of women, even from some of the women themselves. Some of the keys to success included:

- Identifying common objectives and coherent strategies based on academic knowledge, political advocacy, and public pressure. This made it possible to overcome prejudice and the cultural and social obstacles that tend to be more difficult than those imposed by law.

- Building an alliance between many different sectors in society – lawyers, academics, politicians, NGOs, and women's groups.

- Realising that small gains were an incentive to keep people engaged and motivated to take on bigger challenges ahead.

- Working with the media, and making links with journalists. It was necessary to identify angles that would interest the press, and use the appropriate language.

- Doing thorough research and understanding the gender inequalities on which the law was based.

- Having a sound legal basis for the proposal. ADC commissioned studies from legal experts that grounded the proposal firmly in legal knowledge and expertise.

- Ensuring that the leadership, especially women's leadership, had the resources to identify situations of gender discrimination and to be convinced both of the need to remove this discrimination and of the feasibility of doing so.

There is more work to be done in this area. Many women in Peru still do not know about the changes to the law, especially in remote and rural areas. More research is needed on how it is affecting the lives of children and of single mothers. The law must be made retrospective so that it applies to children who still have both their mother's surnames.

At the time of writing, the campaign continues and the Alliance is lobbying RENIEC (the public institution in charge of documentation in Peru) to try to build the capacity of civil registrars at the national level. The campaign wants civil registrars to be informed of key facts, such as that the procedure to register a child is free; that single mothers should not have to pay a fee; and that the father should be notified of any new procedures.

There are many other policies that discriminate against women and poor people in Peru, which infringe their rights and silence their voices. Changing these will take time, but it is a task that civil society, international co-operation, and progressive sectors of the state can embark on together. For now, one small battle has been won.

Notes

[1] UNICEF (2005) 'Child protection from violence, exploitation and abuse: Desmond Tutu helps launch campaign for Universal Birth Registration', www.unicef.org/protection/index_25228.html (last accessed September 2008).

[2] UNICEF (n.d.) 'Child protection from violence, exploitation and abuse: Birth Registration', www.unicef.org/protection/index_birthregistration.html (last accessed September 2008).

[3] *Ibid.*

[4] *Ibid.*

[5] UNICEF (2007) 'Progress for Children: A World Fit for Children, Statistical Review', Number 6, www.unicef.org/progressforchildren/2007n6/files/ Progress_for_Children_-_No._6.pdf (last accessed September 2008).

[6] UNICEF (n.d.) *op.cit.*

[7] *Ibid.*

[8] According to the Instituto Indigenista Interamericano III, cited in National Vital Statistics and Civil Registry Office (RENIEC) (2005) 'National Plan to Restore Identity: Documenting the Undocumented 2005–2009', Perú.

[9] UNDP (2007) 'Peru – The Human Development Index – Going Beyond Income', http://hdrstats.undp.org/countries/country_fact_sheets/ cty_fs_PER.html (last accessed September 2008).

[10] Desarollo Peruano, http://desarrolloperuano.blogspot.com/2008/06/el-per-en-el-ranking-latinoamericano_08.html (last accessed September 2008).

[11] Figures from the National Plan to Restore Identity (2005), approved by the National Vital Statistics and Civil Registry Office (RENIEC), the constitutional body responsible for civil registries in Peru.

[12] See Mountain Voices, www.mountainvoices.org/p_th_gender.asp #testimonies (last accessed September 2008).

[13] R. Mendoza (2006) 'Niños deben tener sus dos apellidos', *La República* www.larepublica.com.pe/component/option,com_contentant/task,view/id,105 930/Itemid,0/; and Diary of Debates, Second Session of Congreso 2005 (30 March 2006), pp. 136–7, www2.congreso.gob.pe/sicr/diariodebates/ Publicad.nsf/SesionesPleno?OpenView&Start=1&Count=30&Expand=6.5.1 #6.5.1 (last accessed September 2008).

[14] Article 2 (inc. b) of the Constitution of Peru.

Cover photograph: María Inés Aragonés/Mesa de Concertación de Lucha contra la Pobreza (Alliance against Poverty), 2006

Oxfam GB

Oxfam GB is a development, relief, and campaigning organisation that works with others to find lasting solutions to poverty and suffering around the world. Oxfam GB is a member of Oxfam International.

Oxfam House
John Smith Drive
Cowley
Oxford
OX4 2JY
Tel: +44.(0)1865.473727
E-mail: enquiries@oxfam.org.uk
www.oxfam.org.uk

11. Keep Your Promises

Campaigning to hold government to account in India

Activists highlight the difference in scale between promises and delivery.

Despite its booming economy and burgeoning middle classes, India is a country where hundreds of millions remain in severe poverty. In 2004 a new government was elected largely due to its promise to improve the lives of the poorest and most marginalised people by creating health centres, schools, and jobs. Also in 2004, the World Social Forum in Mumbai brought a diverse range of Indian organisations together, who later formed Wada Na Todo Abhiyan, the 'Keep Your Promises' campaign, to ensure a collective movement for change. This paper explains how the campaign succeeded in mobilising hundreds of thousands of people in India to pressure the government to deliver on key promises, and in demonstrating the huge demand of people across India for social justice and a better future for all the nation's children.

Introduction

India has long been a country of contradictions. The country boasts the largest number of billionaires in the world.[1] Its economy is booming, and it is seen as a hotspot for global investors. But it is also home to at least 25 per cent of the world's poor people. One in every three illiterate people in the world lives there,[2] at least 35 million children aged six to 14 do not attend school, and the country accounts for more than 20 per cent of global maternal and child deaths.[3] It comes close to the bottom of the list in the 2007/8 United Nations Human Development Report, at 128 out of 177 countries. It is a country of huge inequalities, where poor and marginalised people are among the most deprived in the world.

In 2004, the United Progressive Alliance (UPA) won the elections and formed a government. Its coming to power was largely due to its promises in its election manifesto to meet the aspirations of the large masses of poor and marginalised people under what was known as the national 'Common Minimum Programme', or CMP. These promises included raising expenditure on education from 3 to 6 per cent of gross domestic product (GDP), and expenditure on health from less than 1 per cent to 2 to 3 per cent.

Since then, the government has rolled out key flagship schemes for education, health, and livelihoods. These include the National Rural Health Mission to expand health care for rural poor people; and the National Rural Employment Guarantee Scheme, which provides 100 days' employment a year on demand, as a right, for rural households whose adult members volunteer to do unskilled manual work.[4] The government has also promised to look into the needs of marginalised groups like Dalits (formerly known as 'untouchables', who are outside the caste system and considered to be unworthy to enter the social and religious life of society), indigenous peoples, religious minorities, and women.

In the same year that the new government was elected, civil-society groups gathered in Mumbai for the World Social Forum to articulate a joint agenda focusing on governance and accountability, asking the government to deliver on key promises to poor people. A core group of 40 organisations was involved in the process, which emerged as Wada Na Todo Abhiyan (WNTA – also known as the 'Keep Your Promises' Campaign). Its thematic focus was on livelihoods, education and health, and social exclusion. It was to be a watchdog on the government's progress. Its aim was to give a collective voice to disparate movements across the country by joining them under one unified umbrella.

Oxfam, as a founding and very active board member of WNTA, played an important role in supporting the alliance, and fellow members of the alliance were very clear that they wanted Oxfam's involvement to go well beyond funding. In particular, Oxfam was the key resource for research and policy analysis, for media and communications and events support, and for facilitating lobbying and advocacy. At the same time, however, Oxfam made a deliberate decision not to use the campaign to highlight Oxfam's own brand. WNTA's convenor, Amitabh Beher, confirms this, noting, appreciatively, 'Oxfam has participated not in the style of donor but as one of the constituents, ready to subsume the Oxfam identity within the campaign identity and work passionately for the campaign'.

From small beginnings

The success of WNTA has been spectacular. Since 2004, it has grown from a small idea to a large organisation with a federal structure reaching 23 states. It has 3,000 networks and a core membership of 105 organisations. Initially, no one believed that a national coalition of this size would really come together and be taken seriously by the government. But the organisers planned well. From the beginning, it was envisaged that as well as creating a national advocacy agenda, emphasis would also be on decentralised state-level campaigns to ensure that local priorities were included. The focus was not on setting up a 'super body', but on harnessing and bringing together what already existed at all levels in Indian society.

What the campaign has done

The campaign focused on three main areas – livelihoods, education and health, and social exclusion.

Its programmes have included:

- Public awareness and action on the National Rural Employment Guarantee Act and Scheme, National Rural Health Mission, and the Right to Education Bill.

- The 'Nine Is Mine' campaign for the allocation of 9 per cent of GDP to health and education, as promised in the CMP.

- Civil-society reviews of the CMP in May 2007, in particular looking at gender and caste issues.

- Release of the Citizens' Reports on the Millennium Development Goals (MDGs) in December 2006.

- Advocacy with legislators on livelihoods, health, and education.

- A People's Summit Against Poverty (PSAP) in September 2005, involving more than 12,000 people.

WNTA is also the national partner of the Global Call for Action against Poverty (GCAP) and has directly engaged with United Nations systems, especially the Millennium Campaign.

11. Keep Your Promises, Speaking Out, Programme Insights, Oxfam GB. November 2008.

2

Ashok Bharti, convenor of the National Conference of Dalit Organisations, a network of over 300 groups, and also the national convenor of WNTA's steering group, says: 'Wada Na Todo Abhiyan, which works around the issues of governance and accountability, has not only provided Dalits and other marginalised sections with a civil-society platform to collectively raise their issues and concerns with the government, policy makers, and other institutions of governance and accountability, but has also helped them to share their experiences with the wider society and hence compelled them to look critically even at their own programmes focusing on governance and accountability'.[5]

Three strategies

From the very beginning, WNTA used three strategies: mass mobilisation, policy audits and citizens' reports, and budget tracking and advocacy. These involved direct engagement with marginalised groups such as Dalits, women, indigenous (*adivasi*) peoples (referred to by the government as 'tribals'[6]), children, and people with disabilities.

Mass mobilisation

WNTA has repeatedly managed to organise events with a large and active mass presence and extensive media coverage. In the very first year, it organised a People's Summit Against Poverty, which was supported by major political parties and even the members of the Planning Commission, the principal constitutional body responsible for planning the development process in India. A People's Charter calling for immediate action to meet the MDG commitments and end poverty was set out. These were not merely rhetorical calls to end poverty; they were related to specific actions mandated by the people.

WNTA has regularly staged mass protests on 17 October, global 'Stand Up Against Poverty' day. On that day in 2007, WNTA partners across 15 states organised a diverse set of actions involving 1,236,979 people from communities and *panchayats* (local decision-making bodies), including students and government representatives. These actions were designed to remind the government to fulfil its commitment to end poverty and social exclusion, as promised in the United Nations Millennium Declaration and India's National Development Goals.[7]

The campaign has also actively involved children in campaigning for health and education spending. The children bring an energy and freshness to the campaign. When they ask questions of government, it is difficult for politicians to avoid giving a straight answer. The children even met the Prime Minister. The children's alliance mixes children from slums and those from wealthy cities. Some have very little or no education, others are much better educated and comfortably off, but are concerned and aware of the country's inequalities and have a real sense of empathy. It is basically a cross-class alliance for social justice; a vision for the future of India.

The link between mass mobilisation, media coverage, and access to decision-makers was clear. After the campaign got schools across the country involved through grassroots mobilisation, an inspired (and inspiring) teacher volunteered to work with the campaign to organise a concert in the national stadium and a children's rally. Everyone pitched in. When thousands of children – from the poorest slums and the most elite Delhi schools – attended the concert and rally, dancing together and marching side by side, the media rushed to cover this unusual social phenomenon on TV. The day after the TV coverage, the Prime Minister's office invited the children to come and meet him. And when they met him, he accepted the 100,001st postcard petition and assured the children, on the record, that he would boost funding for schools and health centres. In the following budget, he did just that, raising health spending by a quarter and education spending by a third in a budget in which defence spending went up by just 9 per cent. The increases in health and education were still not enough to fill the historical shortfall or fully meet the government's promises, but analysts agreed that they were larger than they would ever have been without civil-society pressure.

Children as leaders: 'Nine is Mine'

The 'Nine is Mine' campaign was led by children across the country. The 'nine' refers to the 6 per cent of GDP on education plus the 3 per cent on health that the children claim as their right. The campaign was launched on 16 October 2006 in Delhi, and over 4,500 children participated from ten states. A nationwide petition was launched. A statement on the petition said: 'We are the children of India. We are not voters, but we believe that the voices of children can be stronger than the votes of adults. And we know that it is necessary for us to speak up now to secure our future'.

Consistent and wide mainstream media coverage ensured that the Prime Minister met a delegation consisting of 20 children to listen to their demands and assure them of his support. About 80 MPs were briefed about the demand through various partner delegations.

On 13 November 2007, the 300,001st signature was signed in the presence of Planning Commission member Abhijit Sen and handed over to him to be passed on to the finance minister. The next day, children also met the Chairperson of the Child Rights Commission, seeking her support for their demands.

The second phase of the campaign, from November 2007 to January 2008, has seen increased activity, with 5,000 signatures being sent off to the finance minister each day. An indicator of the enthusiasm the movement has generated among children comes from 14-year-old Yayabangarababu, who said: 'I'm in Delhi to listen and to talk about our rights. I am here to urge the government to keep its promises for better education and health. I am here to make sure that those in power give the promised 9 per cent of the GDP for the children of this country'.

> When the Five-Year Plan for 2008 to 2012 was approved by the government, it tripled the total outlay on education, aiming at a target of 6 per cent by the end of the period.

Policy audits and citizens' reports

In order to press for the full implementation of the National Rural Employment Guarantee Scheme (NREGS), which aims to provide 100 days' employment a year for rural households, WNTA organised a *Rozgar Adhikar Yatras* ('March for the Right to Employment') in six states. These marches were accompanied by People's Tribunals, where local officials were told about the inefficiencies and gaps in the implementation of the scheme. Following this, a National Tribunal was held at the India Social Forum in October 2006, where over 50 representatives from 14 states spoke. The outcomes and verdicts of these processes were taken to different parliamentarians on the first anniversary of the NREGS. This led to further intensification of a 'social audit' of the scheme, which examines the impact of specific government activities on certain sections of society. Although many gaps remain in implementation, the government has acknowledged the importance of the campaign by integrating the audits in its monitoring mechanisms and also increasing the reach of the NREGS to 595 districts from the initial 200.

WNTA used the idea of citizens' report cards to put constant pressure on the government and to hold them to account. In its first year, WNTA brought out a report focusing on the MDGs, particularly in relation to education, health, and employment. A survey involving the local community was conducted in 1,514 villages, which was then released at the Poverty Summit in September 2005. It was followed by a mid-term MDGs checklist and a status report card in July 2007 which was presented to the Prime Minister. Extensive media coverage had titles like 'UPA [United Progressive Alliance – the party of government] secures only 30 per cent marks in People's Report Card' and 'UPA Report Card has Red Marks', which succinctly sent the message home. The current survey involves 10,000 people from 17 states across 100 districts.

Among WNTA's most important annual events has been its review of the CMP. This checks on the major promises made by the government through a rigorous process where experts and groups working on a range of issues like local governance, education, health, land rights, employment, and so on, develop a report card to pick out the positives and negatives. The report is then presented and passed through various state networks to get their feedback and assent before it is finally released. Increasing numbers of people are involved – in the second review in 2006, 250 people from 12 states participated, while in 2007, 400 people from 23 states took part and feedback was taken from over 500 organisations. An elephant showing 'CMP Promised' and a goat showing 'CMP Delivered', illustrating the difference in scale, became a popular image widely used by the media.

Budget tracking and advocacy

The third strategy involved a new and different way of looking at budgets. The budget exercise normally projected by the media is all about cuts in income and sales tax on consumer durables, which mainly affect the middle classes. The media rarely focuses on social-sector issues like health and education that affect the vast mass of poor people.

The Centre for Budget and Governance Accountability (CBGA), a member of the WNTA alliance, has led on providing direct inputs to the campaign on budget tracking and advocacy. Each year, in November (when the government's budget-making process begins for the next year), it organises a National Consultation, and creates a People's Charter of Demands, looking at various aspects of the social sector like agriculture, education, and health from the perspective of marginalised groups. This is forwarded to various ministries of the government. A follow-up is then organised, consisting of a quick yet informed reaction by experts, and a public discussion where government, policy makers, civil-society groups, and media representatives come together to evaluate the implications of the Charter for poor people. The campaign is promoting the right to be heard in an innovative way, where policy analysis from the top has led to grassroots mobilisation from the ground.

Giving a voice to the marginalised

As mentioned above, while the framework of the movement has been to build the capacity of the people to mobilise themselves around the demands of basic rights, there has also been a focus on bringing in the voices of those who are particularly marginalised. This includes a whole range of people such as Dalit groups, women's groups, and indigenous people or 'tribal' groups.

The WNTA wanted to harness the work that these groups were already doing on the issues on which WNTA was mobilising. So, for example, Dalit and women's groups were often focused on issues of exploitation and violence, and WNTA hoped to add to their strength and capacity by including them in its quest to secure their economic rights as well. In this way, it hoped to build both individual and community awareness of these broader issues.

11. Keep Your Promises, Speaking Out, Programme Insights, Oxfam GB. November 2008.

6

Who are the Dalits?

The caste system in India was abandoned by law in 1949, but continues today in many parts of the country. Dalits, formerly known as 'untouchables', are considered by caste Hindus to be outcasts. Traditionally, they worked in trades considered 'unclean' because they were associated with death or animals – such as leather workers, cobblers, scavengers, sweepers, cremation workers, drummers, and removers of animal carcasses. This resulted in physical segregation (for example, not being allowed to drink from the same cup as higher caste people), social segregation, and debt bondage. There are approximately 179 million Dalits in India today – around 20 per cent of the population. They face high levels of illiteracy, poverty, and landlessness. Prejudice means that Dalits are often discriminated against and victimised. A 2005 government report states that a crime is committed against a Dalit every 20 minutes, but this often goes unreported and rarely results in a conviction.

The two major Dalit organisations, the National Consultation on Dalit Human Rights (NCDHR) and the National Conference of Dalit Organisations (NACDOR), organise around the exploitation and especially the physical oppression of Dalits. It is through the WNTA network that they have now cast their net wider on issues of basic services like education and health, and their share in the budgets.

Another process in this regard has been to look at the CMP through the lens of these groups. A report called 'Fulfilling the Promise to End Social Exclusion – A Review of the Dalit Agenda in the National Common Minimum Programme'[8] was launched at the Indian Parliament, asking for key policy changes from a Dalit perspective.

Similarly, a paper entitled 'Gender and Governance – A Review of the Women's Agenda in the National Common Minimum Programme'[9] was released on 8 March 2007, International Women's Day. Twenty-seven events were organised across ten states involving 12,000 people through the national network of women's organisations. On the occasion of 'Stand Up Against Poverty' day in 2007, a 'Women's Tribunal Against Poverty' was organised in which 400 women from 20 states participated to narrate their stories. Nijhula Kachua, one of the participants, drew attention to the plight of labourers and their families in the tea gardens of Assam. She highlighted the fact that these people had little awareness of and almost no access to national government schemes that were operational in other Indian states. The tribunal's final outcomes were presented to the first woman President of India, Pratibha Patil.

Since these successful events, there has been follow-up to the tribunal. International Women's Day 2008 was celebrated by WNTA partners across 44 districts in 11 states of India, bringing together more than 10,000 women. Between 6–17 March 2008, the partners released the 'Women's Charter Against Poverty', which reinforced the demand for women's access to power, resources, and services (originally articulated in the tribunal). This charter also contributed to a national report called 'Divided Destinies: Unequal Lives –

Economic, Social, and Cultural Rights in the Indian State, NGO Report to the UN Committee on Economic, Social, and Cultural Rights'.[10]

WNTA has also addressed gender in its own structures: in 2006, the WNTA steering group was expanded to ensure women made up 50 per cent of members. A specific task force was formed to steer the movement's future course of action on gender.

Successes and future plans

The campaign has had a number of successes at local and national levels.

In 2007, the budget for health was increased by 25 per cent and the budget for education was increased by 33 per cent, while the defence budget went up by just 9 per cent.[11] The education minister is planning to make the right to education a fundamental enforceable right. He wants to introduce a Bill towards the end of 2008.

The campaign now has weight with politicians – members are actively invited to give feedback and hold discussions, where two years ago this would never have happened.

Between July 2008 and January 2009 the campaign is organising a 'People's Manifesto', mobilising 300 parliamentary constituents, including MPs, civil-society organisations, and citizens. The main political party knows that this plan is under way and that it is being carried out in collaboration with three major TV channels. Education and health are now high up the political agenda and they are now seen as human-rights issues.

Challenges

One of the major challenges of managing such a large platform is, predictably enough, to keep all the constituent parts on an equal footing and to ensure that they present a united front. This has been possible through giving different groups leadership on different issues; for example, while one group concentrates on economic rights, the other focuses on educational rights.

The campaign drew in a very wide range of different groups across ethnic, caste, class, and political divides. It was not only a campaign of already active citizens, but also a campaign that inspired those who normally wouldn't think of themselves as activists but merely as people who cared about their children's and the country's future. The main challenge at the start was to get such a disparate group of people and organisations working well together. People were very aware of their differences. Building joint alliances around the issues and concerns of marginalised people has not been easy. In particular,

11. Keep Your Promises, Speaking Out, Programme Insights, Oxfam GB. November 2008.

8

it has been a challenge to involve the middle classes, who were initially reluctant to join up with activist groups, and sceptical about a campaign that called on government to spend more money on government schools and health centres that middle-class Indians do not themselves use. But by explaining the campaign in terms of giving all children a chance, and of enabling all Indians to contribute to the country's development, the campaign was able to dent some of that scepticism.

Over the years, trust has built up between alliance members. Now when they discuss what needs to be done, they know that they are all collectively responsible, and so work together to achieve what they want. People are much more aware of what they have in common: a commitment to social justice in India.

At regional state level it has been more of a mixed experience. In some states, groups divided into factions, each of which wanted to dominate the state secretariat. Problems at state level are not helped by the fact that while there is intense and ongoing interaction at the national level, states usually only galvanise at key moments instead of being part of a continuing flow, which makes it difficult to keep the momentum going.

This is a challenge, but is especially important for groups working at the grassroots, as they need constant motivation to remain engaged in what is not an easy task. This motivation has to come from an understanding that national work can only succeed when supported at state and local levels.

Key lessons

The campaign has learned a lot in its four years of existence. Some of its key lessons are:

- **Overcoming isolation:** Marginalised groups, for many reasons, tend to work in isolation. Building alliances and overcoming isolation without giving up one's identity, perspective, and sensibility has strengthened the partners' faith in working with civil society.

- **Putting local priorities first:** For any large network to be successful in ensuring poor people's right to be heard, the priorities have first to be drawn from local, regional, and national contexts and then draw on international frameworks.

- **Bringing in different perspectives and voices:** The national framework has to take account of the perspectives and voices of groups that are marginalised in social and economic terms, as well as groups of differing gender and age (for example, children), in order to seek their support and build their capacity.

The campaign has also reached out to the middle classes in order to use their lobbying strength.

- **Seeking common ground:** It is important not to organise separate or new fronts but to look at the opportunities to bring isolated or disparate movements together on common ground, making them a unified and much stronger voice that cannot be ignored by the government. It was very useful, for example, to bring together three major coalitions to work towards the right to universal education on a common platform when there was a call for the Right to Education Bill to be passed as an act of Parliament. Similarly, getting those groups working on budgets and the social sector on a common platform has helped mainstream budget advocacy and made this a core area of concern for many civil-society groups.

- **Building on strong points:** The strong points of each of the constituents must be harnessed for the interest of the whole. Such strengths include, for example, grassroots groups providing input from the ground; policy groups providing macro analysis in a language that is informed by grassroots realities; media-based groups providing support for media advocacy, and so on. One of WNTA's advantages is that different activities can be led by different member organisations according to their areas of strength, building skills and experience in the proces.

- **Using the right language:** It is possible to create excitement and enthusiasm for issues such as health and education. The key is to articulate these vital issues in a language that people understand and want to respond to.

- **Adapting for appropriate contexts:** There is a recognition that the Indian model is specific to the Indian context and is not a 'one size fits all' approach. However, adapting the model for use in other countries could make a real difference to campaigning in developing countries across the world. In the Indian context, the already thriving civil-society movements on people's rights have of course been very helpful, as people didn't need to start from scratch. However, the focus was on rights to health and education, which had *not* previously been the main agenda of most of the organisations. So building on pre-existing foundations and using their strategic inputs is a proven successful strategy for the campaign.

11. Keep Your Promises, Speaking Out, Programme Insights, Oxfam GB. November 2008.

10

Notes

[1] NY Daily News (2008) 'India ranks first in the world in number of billionaires, new Forbes list shows', www.nydailynews.com/news/us_world/2008/03/05/2008-03-05_india_ranks_first_in_the_world_in_number.html (last accessed September 2008).

[2] The Times of India (2004) 'India has a third of world's illiterates', http://timesofindia.indiatimes.com/articleshow/916814.cms (last accessed September 2008).

[3] 'Children in India', www.smilefoundationindia.org/ourchildren.htm (last accessed September 2008).

[4] Ministry of Rural Development, Government of India, 'National Rural Employment Guarantee Act', www.nrega.nic.in/ (last accessed September 2008).

[5] From a speech made at the annual review of the Campaign Co-ordination Meeting of Wada Na Todo Abhiyan, organised in Delhi during April 2008.

[6] A tribe can be defined as a social group which existed before the development of states or which lives outside of states. In terms of socio-economic status they are at the bottom of Indian society. 'Adivasi' is the Hindu word for 'tribals'.

[7] National Development Goals are defined in accordance with the Five-Year Plans undertaken by the Indian government. India is now in its 11th Five-Year Plan phase. See Social Watch India, 'Commitments: MDGs, Common Minimum Programme, National Development Goals', http://socialwatchindia.net/commit_5.htm (last accessed September 2008).

[8] Wada Na Todo Abhiyan (2007) 'Fulfilling the Promise to End Social Exclusion – A Review of the Dalit Agenda in the National Common Minimum Programme', New Delhi: Wada Na Todo Abhiyan.

[9] Wada Na Todo Abhiyan (2007) 'Gender and Governance – A Review of the Women's Agenda in the National Common Minimum Programme', New Delhi: Wada Na Todo Abhiyan.

[10] People's Collective for Economic, Social, and Cultural Rights (2008) 'Divided Destinies: Unequal Lives – Economic, Social, and Cultural Rights in the Indian State, NGO Report to the UN Committee on Economic, Social, and Cultural Rights', New Delhi: People's Collective for Economic, Social, and Cultural Rights. The report was initiated by the Programme on Women's Economic Social and Cultural Rights.

[11] Expenditure Budget Vol. I, Union Budget 2008–09, Government of India.

Cover photograph: K. Satheesh/Tehelka news magazine, Delhi (2007)

Oxfam GB

11. Keep Your Promises, Speaking Out, Programme Insights, Oxfam GB. November 2008.

12

12. The Global Call to Action against Poverty

International voices for change

Examples of the white band worn by GCAP supporters

The Global Call to Action against Poverty (GCAP) is the world's largest civil-society movement calling for an end to poverty and inequality. It has involved millions of people in mass protests and has had some significant successes in changing policies and promises on aid, trade, and development and in articulating the voices of poor and marginalised people. This paper examines the movement's strategies and achievements, and looks at the challenges that remain.

Introduction

The Global Call to Action against Poverty (GCAP) is the world's largest civil-society alliance of social movements, international non-government organisations (NGOs), trade unions, community groups, women's organisations, faith and youth groups, local associations, and campaigners working together across more than 100 national coalitions/platforms to end the structural causes of poverty and inequality.[1] To date, it has involved over 50 million people on every continent of the world[2] calling for action from the world's leaders to meet their promises to end poverty and achieve the Millennium Development Goals.

Mass mobilisation by GCAP raises public awareness of the structural causes of poverty, and strengthens advocacy work at national level. It provides a platform for those living in poverty to take an active part in the political decision-making processes that most affect them.

Each country mounts its own campaign involving thousands of people, so GCAP has taken place in a wide variety of different local contexts, with different political targets, and different constituencies.

GCAP's largest mobilisations have been on 17 October every year; this is International Day for the Eradication of Poverty. Over 47.3 million people took part in the 'Stand Up' campaign on that day in 2007.[3] Many of those who become involved wear a white band to demonstrate the truly worldwide nature of the campaign.

GCAP has been supported by international figures such as Brazilian President Lula da Silva, and Nelson Mandela, who said: 'As long as poverty, injustice and gross inequality persist in our world, none of us can truly rest...The Global Call to Action against Poverty can take its place as a public movement alongside the movement to abolish slavery and the international solidarity against apartheid'.[4]

Furthermore, GCAP is an open platform for organisations and campaigns working on social-justice issues to link in numerous ways. Oxfam supports GCAP globally. At the same time, its national offices are frequently linked with GCAP national coalitions, and GCAP often supports Oxfam's thematic campaigns, particularly at the national level.

This paper outlines a few of the strategies and processes used by GCAP in a number of different countries. It looks at its success in affecting policy change and outlines the challenges facing such a global movement.

From love affair to married couple...a history of GCAP

In September 2003, Graca Machel, international advocate for women's and children's rights, hosted a meeting of NGOs in Maputo, Mozambique, where the idea of GCAP first emerged, supported by prominent civil-society activists such as Civicus Secretary-General Kumi Naidoo. In 2004, GCAP launched a campaign and issued a declaration known as the Johannesburg Declaration.

In 2005, there was a groundswell of activity on the issue of poverty. There was an unprecedented level of involvement from civil society at the Gleneagles G8 summit, a forum whose doors had traditionally been closed to anyone except the heads of the richest states. This involvement resulted in a commitment by the G8 countries to improve the quality and quantity of their aid. The first substantial commitments to debt cancellation were made, and there was a feeling that civil society, by having its voices heard, was able to contribute to policy change on poverty issues in meaningful ways.

In 2006 and 2007, GCAP faced a bit of an identity crisis. The level of response to the Call to Action was so overwhelming that there was unanimous agreement that it was a movement that had to be continued beyond 2005. However, the leading organisations did not have a co-ordinated way of capitalising on this enthusiasm and translating it into steps forward for a global coalition against poverty. As Ana Agostino, co-chair of GCAP, said: 'It's like a passionate love affair; in making our mobilisation plans, we're always trying to relive the enthusiasm, the passion of 2005, and we are going to have to admit that it's not something we can recreate. The political environment has changed, and the hearts and minds of the public have changed. We're now an old, married coalition, and we need to find a way to adjust to our new circumstances'.[5]

GCAP responded by developing its structures, promoting internal learning about the value and role of the coalition, building national coalitions, and solidifying GCAP as a participant in policy-making forums. Global strategies focused on: amplifying actions against poverty led by national coalitions or coalition members at the global level, and mass mobilisation on global days.

Fighting poverty: goals, issues, and structure

GCAP aims are to: 'Fight the structural determinants and causes of poverty and challenge the institutions and processes that perpetuate poverty and inequality across the world', and to 'work for the defence and promotion of human rights, gender equality and social justice'.[6]

Its latest public declaration in 2007, known as the Montevideo Declaration, says: 'We are committed to democratising the values, mechanisms and processes of negotiation and decision making in the interest of the poorest and marginalised people, and to ensuring that equity, human security and inclusion are the core principles around which global, regional and local governance is organised.'[7]

The main issues on which GCAP campaigns include:

- public accountability, just governance, and the fulfilment of human rights

- trade justice

- a major increase in the quantity and quality of aid and financing for development

- debt cancellation

- gender equality

- countering climate chaos.

GCAP has an International Facilitation Team (IFT), in which all regions are represented, and members voice concerns and actions. The IFT represents national coalitions, international organisations, youth and children, workers, and religious constituencies. Similar structures have been established at the regional level, with the Asian, African, and Latin American Facilitation Teams. There are also a variety of task forces. Some are functional, on media, mobilisation, and e-communications, and others are ad hoc, or represent a particular constituency such as children and youth, or women.

Three examples of the way GCAP has worked are women's tribunals, refugee testimonies, and lobbying international financial institutions such as the World Bank and the International Monetary Fund (IMF).

Women's Tribunals: voices for change

GCAP's women's task force organised a series of International Women's Tribunals Against Poverty, highlighting the feminisation of poverty. With women constituting 70 per cent of the world's poor people, the tribunals served to present the testimonies of women on the conditions they face and to put pressure on governments to take action.

For example, the tribunals in Peru took place on 17 October 2007, International Day for the Eradication of Poverty. They aimed to highlight the situation endured by women living in rural areas, who are more vulnerable to poverty and prevented from exercising their rights and citizenship on a daily basis. The cases presented were: issues arising from a lack of official documents, rape in internal armed conflict, rape of indigenous girls, and forced sterilisation.

Bringing these cases to a tribunal made explicit the link between poverty and the violation of human rights. Clear demands were presented to the Peruvian government on issues of documentation, gender-sensitive education, access to contraceptives, and increased legislative and judicial support for survivors of sexual violence and rape.

Other tribunals have taken place in different countries throughout the world where they have proven to be a powerful way of making the voices of marginalised women heard.

The primary challenge encountered by the tribunals is how to link them with ongoing processes of advocacy and policy making in order to bring about change. In part due to the cross-cutting nature of gender-justice issues, targeting key local political opportunities has been difficult, and depending on the local context, GCAP coalitions have struggled to follow up with demands presented to political decision-makers. While Peru had the advantage of support from strong national coalitions already engaged on gender issues, other countries hoping to replicate the model have needed support in linking to ongoing advocacy networks. In Bosnia and Herzegovina, the tribunal proved to be an outreach opportunity for the coalition, strengthening ties to women's-rights activists.

The perspectives from these tribunals were all taken to the Commission on the Status of Women in New York, which took place on International Women's Day 2007. Mobilisation plans for 2008 were launched at the event, and advocacy efforts at the UN focused on the GEAR campaign (UN Gender Equality Architecture Reform).

Ana Agostino, GCAP co-chair, said: 'Numbers tell a story, and the story they tell is about the feminisation of poverty. Women are disproportionately affected by poverty and inequality, and we have so many measures to tell us this. However, what the women's tribunals demonstrate is that poverty is not a number. Poverty is about people, and peoples' lives. We can take a lot from statistics, but we need to be mindful in policy making forums that decisions about numbers, about budgets, are decisions about the way women and men live their lives'.[8]

Refugee testimonies

On 17 October 2007 in South Africa, the GCAP coalition organised 'Refugee Testimonies Against Poverty and Inequality' at the Methodist Church in Johannesburg, in which refugees spoke about their experiences of violence, and lack of access to services. Representatives from the Department of Home Affairs and the police service attended, hearing first-hand people's experiences of lack of documentation, xenophobia, arbitrary detentions, denial of basic services, and other violations of rights, often caused by those with the responsibility to protect and uphold those very rights.

This is what Emmanuel Mulamba, of the Johannesburg Refugee Ministries, said: 'As a refugee in Johannesburg, we face exclusion from all angles. The asylum process is inadequate, and even when we have made successful claims, service providers, banks, employers and others refuse to recognise the legitimacy of our papers. Xenophobia is rampant in the department of home affairs and within the police, meaning that we have nowhere to turn for support. Through the Refugee Testimonies, we have been given the chance to voice our concerns. We don't expect all our problems to be solved, but at least we have started engaging with people who can change this ongoing exclusion. We are raising awareness about xenophobia, and as public attitudes change, we hope to get different treatment from public institutions'.[9]

Only two months after the testimonies were held, police raided the Methodist Church that was serving as a shelter to many homeless refugees, brutalising and illegally detaining hundreds of people. Six months later, waves of xenophobic attacks left over 50 migrants to South Africa dead, and thousands more displaced. Civil-society leaders who took part in the refugee testimonies were key in quelling the rioting and facilitating the reintegration of migrants into their communities.

This case has demonstrated that some of the traditional advocacy tools in GCAP are now inadequate for addressing the needs of the most marginalised people, who in various ways fall outside traditional structures of state accountability and protection.

In the case of South Africa, the policies to promote the rights of refugees are in place, but there is inadequate implementation. This is not a unique situation. As a response, the GCAP coalition is working through the People's Budget Campaign, a civil-society shadow of the national budget, to call for a programme that will create awareness in the public sector of xenophobia and the rights of refugees. This will ensure that the refugee testimonies can speak to people who are empowered to listen to their messages, and make changes. Combining testimonies with advocacy around resource allocation and budgeting is a strategy that some GCAP constituents have used successfully, and more are taking on board as a way of ensuring that people's voices are heard and listened to by those with the power to bring about change.

Lobbying international financial institutions

International financial institutions (IFIs) such as the World Bank and the IMF have been a key political target of GCAP. Throughout GCAP's constituencies, there has been recognition that the conditions of many IMF loans (known as conditionalities) are harmful to vulnerable people. Attention has been brought to this through media work at global and national level, as well as through symbolic actions by activists at the IFI meetings. Grassroots 'ambassadors' affected by the policies of the IFIs have taken part in awareness raising and protest, and mass mobilisation has taken place in both the North and South to call for reform.

However, the room for civil-society engagement to create change has so far been very limited, and many GCAP constituents have failed to find a political 'hook', or target capable of enacting the changes demanded. While voices were being raised against decisions that exacerbated poverty and inequality, they were not being heard by the decision-makers.

This was partly because finding a way of forming national demands has been a challenge. In 2008, the GCAP coalition in Bangladesh protested against the IMF's Policy Support Instrument,[10] which is supposed to enable the IMF to support low-income countries that do not want - or need - financial assistance, but who might still seek advice, monitoring, and endorsement of their economic policies from the IMF. The protestors believed it had conditionalities attached that would be harmful to the most vulnerable populations. In spite of marches, protests, and petitions, decisions were being made behind closed doors. Finally, civil-society activists successfully took the government to the High Court, preventing them from signing the Policy Support Instrument. In the case of Bangladesh, civil society was speaking out, but because the political decisions were being made in a different space, they were not being heard. Litigation was a way of forcing the government to listen to the voices of poor people.

In many countries around the world, as well as at the international level, the legislation in place is pro-poor. However, because of a lack of accountability, laws and agreements are often bypassed. Litigation could prove to be a powerful tool for ensuring that those who are calling for justice are heard by decision-makers.

In another example from Bangladesh, a national Women's Development Policy was passed in February, leading to widespread changes in the gender representation of the public sector, as well as having wider implications for women's rights, such as increased maternity leave. While these policy changes cannot be attributed to one specific intervention, there is no doubt that the collective efforts of women expressing the challenges they face in Bangladesh and throughout the sub-region have contributed to a collective momentum for gender justice. Such popular support for change could not have been created without the drive and awareness raising from those who have the most vested interests in such a change.

> **Personal profiles: some of the people who took part in the 'Stand Up and Speak Out' global mobilisation in 2007[11]**
>
> In Liberia, Jonathan Koffa of Monrovia is a 26-year-old musician and singer on the national scene known as Takun J. He says: 'My message to world leaders, the IMF and the World Bank is that they must do more in the shortest time to right out Liberia's debt without conditions. Liberia has just emerged from over 14 years of war which left all sectors of our country destroyed including infrastructure, economy; educational institutions, health facilities, etc. These leaders must be practical in their pledge to meet the MDGs'.
>
> In Germany, 25-year-old student Katharina Weltecke volunteered for the 'Stand Up and Speak Out' activities planned by the local GCAP campaign, 'Deine Stimme gegen Armut' ('Your voice against poverty'). She believes that no time should be wasted reminding those responsible politically to fulfill the MDGs. 'Governments have to make a greater effort than in the past to eliminate the structural causes of poverty.' Katharina came face to face with the effect of poverty while studying in South Africa where she witnessed the devastating impact of HIV and AIDS.
>
> In Pakistan, Syeda Ghulam Fatima Gillani is a 41-year-old women's-rights activist and trade unionist, and a member of the Bonded Labour Liberation Front, the Citizen Council of Pakistan, and the South Asian Alliance for Poverty Eradication. She believes that the neglect of women in developing countries, especially in Pakistan, is a matter for urgent attention. On 17 October 2007 she was one of the people to hold up the world's longest banner which she signed with her demands. This signed banner was used to remind states of their obligations to eradicate poverty and especially to develop gender equality. It said: 'Please allocate 25 per cent of GDP to provide education, health and training to women, especially in rural areas, to uplift their standard of living. Reduce expenditure on the defence and spend it on the eradication of poverty'.

Achievements and challenges

GCAP has had a part in some other successes over the past few years, including:[12]

- European commitments to increase aid to 0.56 per cent by 2010 and 0.7 per cent by 2015

- renewal of G8 pledges to double aid

- agreement to cancel the debts of 18 heavily indebted poor countries and Nigeria

- a commitment by the G8 that they will no longer force poor countries to liberalise their economies[13]

- numerous national-level policy changes, from the institution of school feeding schemes in Niger, to a more pro-poor health policy in Russia, to a Better Aid bill in Canada.

Most of GCAP's strengths, which have allowed it to achieve its successes, are simultaneously its biggest challenges.

A coalition of the willing

GCAP's effectiveness depends on the activity level and ownership of its members. Without lively and strong national coalitions that are equally led by those living in poverty and supported by informed policy analysis by supporters, GCAP would cease to exist. However, it also means that there is a kind of 'whoever can, does' attitude within GCAP; most activities are taken on by a coalition of the willing. While this is not inherently problematic, in many cases it has led to a de facto division of labour with a significant portion of GCAP work.

Resources and representation

Because of a lack of all kinds of resources, many national coalitions and leaders of socially excluded groups do not have the time and capacity to lead on GCAP activities at the global level. The demographics of many groups leading GCAP activities globally are not always representative of the campaign as a whole. Because they have the resources and technical capacity, a political steer often comes from international NGOs (often Northern-led), rather than the grassroots constituents.

GCAP has instituted a number of measures to address this, including regional, gender-based, and other quotas of representation, and enabling wider participation by looking at creative solutions to the technological and linguistic requirements for participating in discussions. A constituency group of socially excluded peoples is also coming together to have a voice on the global council.

The tribunals that took place in 2007 were also a good model in responding to the challenge of representation. They showed how political leadership on policy issues is created by those living in poverty while still allowing space for those engaged in policy-level debates, and those active in grassroots mobilisation to continue to bring their skills to the table.

Sharing good practices

GCAP is a loose alliance with a diverse base, and it is not unusual for this to create confusion rather than synergy. Decision-making processes can be unclear, lines of communication are easily muddled, and work can be duplicated. In the worst-case scenario, some constituents could undermine the work of others. So far, a strong sense of common purpose has been sufficient to resolve any such conflicts, and most constituencies have developed normalised ways of working between them. Beginning in 2008, a group specifically mandated with facilitating learning between constituencies was created. Because GCAP is so broad, and works in so many different political contexts, sharing good practices internally is a way of strengthening the coalition.

Links

Another challenge for GCAP has been to make explicit the links between popular mobilisation, awareness raising, and policy change. In some cases, this has already been explicit, while in others, a complex variety of factors have contributed to change, and GCAP has had to look broadly at a range of different forms of participation to see which have been the most successful.

Shaping civil-society space

One area where GCAP has achieved increasing success is in working towards creating a norm of civil-society space in a wide range of policy-making forums. At national, regional, and global levels, GCAP is finally in a position that makes it able not only to respond to decisions or react to events but to engage in processes as well. This is not true at all levels, or for all processes, but where it is the case, it has contributed to legitimacy for civil-society participation in a wider array of discussions than before. As a coalition whose constituents have a wide range of views, a clear added value of GCAP is to encourage the creation of space for civil society across the board.

The past three years have demonstrated the need for GCAP to exist globally. Issues affecting poverty and inequality are not isolated, nor do they respect national boundaries. Given the remarkably similar goals of all GCAP constituents, there are few other platforms for taking common actions, showing solidarity, and sharing learning. It remains a challenge to take such an array of different contexts, actions, and results in different countries and harmonise them in such a way that the whole will be greater than the parts.

Notes

[1] GCAP (2007) 'Annual Report 2007', www.whiteband.org/about-gcap/reports/search?SearchableText=annual+AND+report%2A (last accessed September 2008).

[2] This is the author's estimate based on rough figures. It is impossible to have firm numbers for this.

[3] See www.whiteband.org (last accessed September 2008).

[4] 'Nelson Mandela backs Global Call to Action against Poverty', www.whiteband.org/media/gcap-news/archives/gcapnews.2007-04-18.7740150588/?searchterm=nelson%20mandela?searchterm=nelson%20mandela (last accessed September 2008).

[5] From a transcript of a meeting with GCAP Council Chairs, 18 March 2008, Civicus House, Johannesburg, South Africa.

[6] Montevideo Global Meeting, 2007, www.whiteband.org/about-gcap/reports/ift/montevideo-global-meeting-may-2007 (last accessed September 2008). The Montevideo Declaration was issued on 5 May 2007 from the GCAP Assembly held in Montevideo, Uruguay. It was issued by all GCAP national coalitions as the official communiqué of the meeting.

[7] From the GCAP website www.whiteband.org (last accessed September 2008).

[8] From a transcript of a press conference, held on 8 March 2008 (International Women's Day) to launch the GCAP 2008 mobilisation plans. It was held at Constitution Hill in Johannesburg.

[9] From the transcripts of the South African refugee testimonies, held on 17 October 2007 at the Central Methodist Church in Johannesburg.

[10] International Monetary Fund (2007) 'The Policy Support Instrument', www.imf.org/external/np/exr/facts/psi.htm (last accessed September 2008).

[11] www.whiteband.org/media/press-info/regional-personal-profiles-some-of-the-people-taking-part-in-stand-up-speak-out

[12] For more details see www.whiteband.org (last accessed September 2008).

[13] From the Montevideo Declaration, 2007 'Montevideo Global Meeting, 2007', www.whiteband.org/about-gcap/reports/ift/montevideo-global-meeting-may-2007 (last accessed September 2008).

Cover photograph: GCAP 2005

© Oxfam GB, November 2008

This paper was written by Caitlin Blaser. Thank you to Katie Allan and Ciara O'Sullivan for their input and comments on earlier drafts. Thank you also to Nikki van der Gaag who edited the paper and to Emily Laurie who provided research assistance. It is part of a series of papers written to inform public debate on development and humanitarian policy issues. The text may be freely used for the purposes of campaigning, education, and research, provided that the source is acknowledged in full.

For further information please email publish@oxfam.co.uk
Online ISBN 978-1-84814-067-7. This paper is part of a set Speaking Out: How the voices of poor people are shaping the future available for purchase from Oxfam Publishing or its agents, print ISBN 978-0-85598-638-4 for the set of 12 papers. For more information visit
http://publications.oxfam.org.uk/oxfam/display.asp?ISBN=9780855986384

This paper is also available in French and Spanish.

Oxfam GB

Oxfam GB is a development, relief, and campaigning organisation that works with others to find lasting solutions to poverty and suffering around the world. Oxfam GB is a member of Oxfam International.

Oxfam House
John Smith Drive
Cowley
Oxford
OX4 2JY

Tel: +44.(0)1865.473727
E-mail: enquiries@oxfam.org.uk
www.oxfam.org.uk